Giving You the Wow and the How

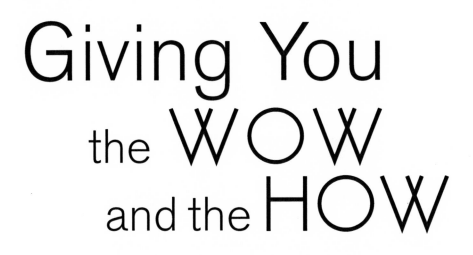

Giving You the WOW and the HOW

44 TIPS From the Millionaire Manicurist that will Change your life Now

Sharmen Lane

New York

Giving You the Wow and the How
44 Tips From the Millionaire Manicurist That Will Change Your Life Now

ISBN 978-1-60037-676-4

Library of Congress Control Number: 2009931650

MORGAN · JAMES
THE ENTREPRENEURIAL PUBLISHER

Morgan James Publishing
1225 Franklin Ave., STE 325
Garden City, NY 11530-1693
Toll Free 800-485-4943
www.MorganJamesPublishing.com

In an effort to support local communities, raise awareness and funds, Morgan James Publishing donates one percent of all book sales for the life of each book to Habitat for Humanity. Get involved today, visit **www.HelpHabitatForHumanity.org**.

Dedication

This book is dedicated to my mother. Thank you for believing in me and always loving and supporting me. It means more to me than you could ever possibly know. I love you.

Acknowledgements

It's amazing how many people influence one little book. There are several people who helped bring this book to life – to all of you I am forever grateful. First my agent, Bill Gladstone this would not have been possible without you. Anne Helliker my editorial consultant. You were instrumental in making this book come to life. My publisher Rick Frishman and David Hancock and all the staff at Morgan James, thank you for all help and support.

My close and dear friends across the globe. I can't possibly mention them all but a few of you are Gregg, Robert, Jeff, Suzi, Erika, Tracy, Aferdita, Masha, Greg, and Sylvia. Each of you has been by my side through this process. Tommy Wagstaff, God rest his soul, I know you were with me every day. You are all close and dear to my heart and I don't know what I would do without you. To everyone who has supported me while making this dream a reality. A special thanks to James and Nubia Eisenlohr of Nubia Photography who did the cover photo. www.nubiaphotography.com.

Testimonials

"This is an energetic inspiring book that gives information to be considered and applied by everyone."

Brian Tracy, *Best-Selling Author and International Speaker*

"Sharmen is a master at connecting with her readers. She breaks down the information with examples that anyone can relate to and apply. I recommend this book for every self-help library!"

Don Hutson, *professional speaker &
Co-author of The One Minute Entrepreneur*

"Sharmen Lane has an energy and message that is powerful for anyone. Her book is insightful and inspiring and empowers us all to make the life we want, happen."

Ethan Willis, *Chief Executive Officer, Prosper, Inc.*

"Sharmen Lane is passionate about passion! Her new book Giving You the Wow and the How really *does* give her readers the WOW and the HOW and what's better than that? Sharmen leads readers step-by-step through the *exact* process she herself used to go from a manicurist to a millionaire. Sharmen gives readers the confidence to believe in their own abilities to achieve whatever it is they desire. This book really *encourages* financial, as well as emotional and spiritual, optimism—and when we are *encouraged,* we have the courage to go out and be, do or have whatever it is we desire. The only thing better for your financial optimism than reading Sharmen Lane's newest book is getting yourself to one of her live speaking events, where her intelligence, enthusiasm and—yes—passion will change the way you see yourself and the possibilities that surround you! Read Sharmen Lane's book and discover for yourself the WOW and the HOW behind creating the life of your dreams!"

Jillian Quinn, *Best-Selling Author of The Secrets of the Bulletproof Spirit: How to Bounce Back from Life's Hardest Hits*

"Sharmen Lane's book delivers a powerful inspirational message that can truly take you into the "Wow Zone." Crafted from empirical knowledge obtained from hard-earned experience, Sharmen delivers big time for those who want to take control of their destiny…NOW!"

Jay Robb, CEO, *motivational speaker, and bestselling author.*

Table of Contents

Introduction

How many times have you taken advice from someone who looked successful and seemed to have all the answers but in reality you really didn't know? Don't you think you should take advice or information from someone who you know has accomplished big things or has already done the things they are telling you to do? Don't you also get frustrated with picking up a book thinking it is going to give you all the answers and when you are finished you realize it was a good read but you had no idea how to apply it to your life? I know I have read just about every book on the shelf about how to change your life. As good as the writer's personal story may have been, where is the *how*? I'm not saying that personal triumph is not important and valuable, it is. However, how did they make it happen? I know at the end of many books, CDs and seminars I am filled with hope and motivation thinking if they can do it so can I! But shortly thereafter I realize I still don't know what to do or how to do it.

Congratulations, this is not that book. Yes, I am going to tell you my story. I'm going to tell you about my life and how I went from being born into the epitome of dysfunction to change my life, overcoming obstacles and adversity to accomplish many great things like making more than a million dollars in one year, running a marathon, personally beating bulimia, starting a charity and much, much more. AND I'm going to tell you what I did and how I did it. Flip through this book right now. In each and every chapter you will see exercises and lessons to walk you through step by step how to get from where you are to where you want to be. This is not just a feel good inspirational story of my life of overcoming adversity; it is a fix-it kit with all the tools you need to do the same. And better yet, you will not only be given the tools but instructions on how to use those tools and examples to get the most out of them.

So why should you listen to me? Because I have been where you are - maybe even worse. But, I moved above and beyond my circumstances. I was born in a small town in Southern California. My parents divorced when I was two years old. I may not remember the divorce, but I do remember the string of bad husbands my mom had after my father left us. I remember the abuse I witnessed and the fear that I always felt in my own home. I remember growing up not having a dad. I remember wondering why he didn't love me and didn't see me when he was only a few hours away. I remember waiting for hours and hours sitting on the curb waiting for him to pick me up for our once or twice a year visit. I remember my dad getting remarried and telling me and my brother that he wasn't going to be around much because his new wife was his top priority and she didn't like kids. I remember how his words stung and how it made for a very sad little girl on Christmas day.

In seventh grade my school psychologist encouraged me to take classes to become a peer counselor. Suddenly, I felt as if I had a purpose in life. I could help others with my new knowledge and past experience. While my peers were reading *Tiger Beat* and *Sassy* I was reading Dale Carnegie, Jim Rohn and Tony Robbins. I was addicted to finding out what made people tick and why. Not surprisingly, this was also the one time my home life was peaceful. My mom was married to a man who was like a father to me. A man who filled that hole my real father had left so many years ago. Unfortunately, the good times came to an end all too soon. After only a few years, he left our lives and more bad men returned. Along with the return of tough times at home came my teenage years. You know the time in your life when you think you know everything.

The time in your life when being popular is the only really important thing. Well, my love for helping others didn't put me in with the popular crowd so I abandoned it. Abandoning that which made me strong was my first mistake in a long string of mistakes to follow.

Being a typical high school teenager I wanted to be part of the "in crowd". I tried out for the cheerleading squad. After a year of hard work and practice, I didn't make it and everyone knew. Then my mother's abusive and humiliating husband died and we moved to a new city. I had to start at a new school in the middle of my sophomore year feeling like a freshman all over again. I knew no one at this school or in this city, which was even smaller than the one I just left. Since I didn't make the cheerleading team I had a back up plan. Between my junior and senior year I went to manicuring school. At 17 I got my manicuring license and started working in a nail salon part time. Even part time I was making more money than my peers had ever even dreamed of. Heck, I was making more money than I had ever thought possible. Remember, I was 17. I had the world figured out, or so I thought. I dropped out of high school just a few months before I was to graduate. I didn't know it then, but dropping out of high school was my second mistake. Doing so was simply continuing the cycle from which I so desperately wanted to break free.

Out on my own, in the real world, I had a taste of what I thought was the good life and I wanted more. I was sure I could do anything I set my mind to. That was until I tried to join the US Air Force. I thought the Air Force would be a glamorous lifestyle. Living in exotic places and most importantly being on my own and free. But the Air Force wouldn't take me without a high school diploma. Then, and only then, did I realize the gravity of the mistake I had made a few years earlier. Sure I thought I had it all figured out. A license to do nails – I didn't need a high school diploma. But, the truth was, I wasn't even allowed to serve my country without that little piece of paper. What had I done? I had thought I was so smart. I thought I had broken free when the truth was I was no further along in life than where I had started.

Determined to turn things around I enrolled in night school and I got my high school diploma. But it was too late for me and the Air Force. That one failure in life had put me in a tailspin. If I had been so wrong about dropping out of high school then what else in my life had I made the wrong decision about? Needless to say, I didn't pursue the Air Force any further after I received my high school diploma. I couldn't. I was too embarrassed to step back into that recruiter's office and admit that I could have been so wrong. So, I continued with my life as a manicurist. A little wounded, but still with a glimmer of hope – because, after all, I did now have my high school diploma. The golden ticket.

By the time I was 22 I had had enough with being a manicurist. Sure it provided me with a glamorous life at 17, but by 22 I wanted more. I was starting to realize that no matter how hard I worked I was never going to make more than $50,000 a year. And there was still that burning desire inside me to make a difference with my life. I figured a change of scenery was just what I needed so I packed up my life and moved from Southern to Northern California. In Northern California I got myself a job as a temp at MCI. I was living the high life again.

About a year after I started at MCI I was up for a promotion. And boy did I want that promotion. I knew that if I got it my life would be back on track. Break that cycle. That was all I could think about. I worked myself to the bone. I went that extra mile and more. Working late for no pay. Showing my dedication to the company in every way that I could. The slap of reality came when someone else got the job instead of me. A girl who was hired from outside the company. And, what was worse, she was told to consult me if she needed help. I wasn't good enough for the job, but I was good enough to train the girl they had hired. What had I done wrong? I was told that I was passed up because of my poor performance on the job, but that couldn't be true. I was good at my job. After all, he did want me to train the girl they had hired. I started to look back at my life – at the things that had held me back before. I became convinced that the reason I was passed up for the promotion was because I didn't go to college. Everyone at that company had gone to college except for me, and everyone knew it.

Was my lack of education going to hold me back for my entire life? Wasn't a lot of hard work and dedication good enough? I figured if they were going to dwell on a few small weaknesses and were not willing to look at all my strengths then they didn't deserve me. I wasn't going to let them tell me what I was worth. I quit that job and started working for a mortgage company. Also, ever learning from my mistakes, four nights a week and Saturday mornings I went to college to get my degree.

Working for the mortgage company, still searching for the dream, I started to think about owning real estate. Owning my own place – that was a sure way of breaking the cycle I so desperately needed to break. If I owned my own home then I would never have to rely on anyone but myself.

I sat down with my boss, crunched a few numbers and realized I was short. Again, I was devastated. But, I had never really been one to let the word "no" stop me. Sure I had had my setbacks, but I never truly accepted no for an answer. If no was the answer I found another way to get a yes. If no was still the answer, then I would simply find a different yes. In order to get my hands on some real estate I took on a second job as a waitress at Denny's – graveyard shift.

Let me tell you, working the graveyard shift at Denny's was not the highlight of my life. What got me through was knowing it was simply a means to an end. It took about three months, but my hard work paid off and I was able to buy a condo. I had done it. At 24 years old I was a homeowner. I was learning from the mistakes of my past, working through them and starting to really control my own destiny. Things were starting to feel possible for me. I had this sudden surge of energy. I could do anything I put my mind to.

At this point in my life I was only 26 and felt I had so much life to live. I wanted to really make a difference. Working for the mortgage company I had seen that the people in sales were making more money than I ever dreamed of. More importantly, they weren't any smarter than me and sure weren't working any harder. In fact, some were barely working 4 hours in a day. I was working more than 40 hours a week. I just imagined what I could do if I got into sales and worked only half as hard as I already was. So what if I had no sales experience? The long tough road of my first 26 years taught me that all it took was a little dedication and determination. I could teach myself to do anything.

Tip #1- Difficult times make you stronger

I applied for a retail mortgage sales position and got it. I hated the job, but I knew in order to find the sales job I really wanted I was going to have to get a little experience under my belt. So, I stuck it out for six months. I knew I could do at least that much. Heck, I had worked the graveyard shift at Denny's for three months. I could do anything. Then, when I heard of an opening with a wholesale mortgage company I applied immediately. I had the experience, I had the gusto, and they had to want me. But they were already looking at someone seriously for the position. Never taking no for an answer I pushed and pushed and got them to finally give me an interview. Needless to say, I got the job.

My first day on the job was a gut wrenching experience. There was no one there to train me. I was thrown into the lion's den and told to sink or swim. I knew I could do this though. I had been thrown into unbeatable situations in the past and for the most part had come out on top. Sure, I might have stumbled a little here and there, but I always worked my way through any situation. So I hunkered down. I listened and I learned and I did. I worked myself to the bone like I knew I could. And, I excelled, like I knew I would. Over the next eight years I made nearly four million dollars in personal income. One year I made just under 1.2 million. I had arrived!

During those eight years there was still a little nagging voice in my head. A little voice that kept telling me, through the years, to never give up. Only, this time the voice was singing a different tune. This time she was telling me that something was missing in my life. How could anything be missing if I was making so much money? I had the life I had never dreamed possible. I owned my own home, I drove an expensive car that I paid cash for, I was debt free, and I was making tons of money. But, I couldn't shake this feeling that the job was going to be the death of me. I wasn't living for me anymore. I was living for the job and the lifestyle it provided. I had to quiet the voice so I started to really look at and analyze my life. Throughout my life I had learned that looking at and analyzing my past helped me to secure my future. Sometimes it was correcting a past mistake and sometimes it was remembering doing something I loved. One thing I new for sure — taking a chance always paid off for me.

Tip #2- Sometimes when you shoot, you'll miss. But sometimes you will score.

It was at that time that my boss asked me to fill in for her as a speaker on a panel. Sure I was nervous, but like I said, I knew that taking a chance had worked for me in the past. This chance was sure to open a door for me somewhere. I hadn't spoken in front of anyone since my school days. Before it was my turn to speak I had the typical, sweaty palms, palpitating heart and quick breathing. But something happened while I was up there for those 10 minutes in front of more than 100 people. A calm and coolness came over me. A confidence that I didn't remember I had washed over me and I delivered the best speech of all the panelists. When I was done I was high as a kite. I was truly elated! It was almost like falling in love. You know, that euphoric feeling when you first meet someone. Where had this come from? And why did it feel so strangely familiar?

I walked around puzzled for a few days at the strange sense of de ja vu I was having. But also bound and determined to feel it again. It came to me at 3 AM one morning. I woke up in a start. Seventh grade. The one time in my childhood where everything was right. My home life was on track, I was working as a peer counselor and I gave an oral presentation in class. Knowing the power of analyzing my past I started to think, and look around me and write things down. It all came to me in a rush.

I knew I loved to speak in public. At one point in my life I had a talent for helping others. My teachers had seen it. Heck I had every self help book known to man on my book shelves at home. I was always the one hired to train the new recruits in any job I had. People were always asking me for advice. How did I always make it to number one in the office, division and many times the company? What did I do so differently?

I took everything I had learned and all the tools I had honed for advancing my own life over the past 20 years and I started to think of how I had already applied them in my life. Although I didn't realize it at the time, using these tools was how I obtained my high school diploma, how I bought my own home, how I excelled to the top of my company in the mortgage business. Knowing what I was doing this time I applied these tools to every aspect of my life. Personal, professional, financial, physical, you name it. That is how I lost 30 pounds. And, that year, that is how I first made more than a million dollars.

I had to share what I had done with everyone around me. I needed to get my secrets for success out there. I needed to empower others to turn their lives around just as I had done.

By the time I turned 32 I was doing fewer mortgages and more speeches. I was speaking every weekend. No matter how tired or cranky I was, when I was speaking I felt revived and alive. It was my job that was weighing me down. Sales wasn't my passion in life, speaking and empowering others was. This was a tough pill for me to swallow, but I realized money wasn't everything. Making more of it wasn't necessarily the answer. The answer was helping others. I also realized I had needed to go through all those steps in my life. They were lessons to me —ways to help me hone my tools for success so that I could share them with others.

By 33 I had gone from liking my job to hating it. What I loved was speaking, training and coaching. That year I retired from corporate

America to follow my passion in life. To help others be, do and have everything they want. To empower people to create the life they always dreamed of. A life they never thought possible. My first year speaking full time I made nearly as much as I had writing mortgages. Making a million in the mortgage business didn't happen over night. As a matter of fact, it took me five years to make a million in one calendar year. But speaking part time, I made the same amount in just my first year as I had my first year in the mortgage business. Again, I had repeated the process I already knew worked. The process that I had been coaching to myself and others almost my entire life. I set a goal, I made a plan and I made it happen.

Tip #3-Life rewards action.

Ever since I left the mortgage business I have taken my passion, incorporated it into my life and found a way to make money doing it. Now I am giving these secrets to others so they can do the same.

Yes, I was born into a life of dysfunction. I didn't tell you my story to make you feel sorry for me. Feeling sorry doesn't do any good. I told you these things so that you know there is always a way out. You can find the silver lining in your life. You can learn to love yourself, your life and above all be successful. Even if you came from nothing. I came from there, but I didn't let it consume me. I turned my life around and so can you. Sure, I have made mistakes along the way. But, I learned from those mistakes. And, hopefully I can teach you through my mistakes. None of us are doomed to repeat the cycle of our upbringing. I am Sharmen Lane and I am here to help you go from now to wow and I am going to show you how.

Chapter 1:
Making the Change

In my early twenties I was floating through life, living day to day with no real goals or passion. I wasn't happy, but I didn't know why. Having no high-school diploma I did the only thing I felt I could. I began working as a manicurist making $20,000 a year though I longed for something more. Yet it seemed that no matter what I did, I still felt stuck. I felt doomed to repeat the life I had seen growing up. Daily, I wrote in my journal asking how I could take my life to the next level. I jumped at every opportunity for something different. I worked as an executive assistant, a receptionist, and even a phlebotomist. Still nothing challenged me. I knew what I was doing wasn't what I wanted, but I also didn't know what I wanted. I read every self-help book I could for inspiration on how to escape the life that I was born into. Until it occurred to me that in order to change my life, I needed to stop feeling trapped by my upbringing. I had to ask myself the tough questions, and make myself hear the answers. It was up to me to make the change.

This realization first occurred when I was 12 years old, and in the seventh grade, I found myself talking to the school psychologist. Actually, I was complaining to him about my home life and how badly I wished it would change. I remember him looking at me and saying

"Sharmen, the only person who can change your life is you." I was taken aback and thought, "How is that possible? I'm only 12 years old! How in the world am I going to change things at home or anywhere else, for that matter?"

He went on to ask me specific questions relating to the problems, as well as exactly what I wanted to change and why. My answers were typical of someone my age at the time and mostly involved complaints about my lack of freedom, the fact that my mother didn't seem to trust me, a desire for a later curfew and displeasure with what seemed to be an extensive list of things I was not allowed to do. "Sharmen," he said, "we aren't always able to control other people, but what we can control is how we react to them." Well, then I was even more confused. My young mind wasn't able to wrap itself around the concept of how changing my reactions was going to be of any help to changing the overall situation. "How is that supposed to change things?!" I wanted to scream.

Yet, when I went home that day I couldn't get his advice out of my head. As if on cue, my mother came home from work and discovered I hadn't completed one of my assigned chores and oh boy was I in trouble. Just as I was about to snap back with a sarcastic response, the school psychologist's words crept back into my head and I thought "I can only change the way I respond." I stopped myself and I concentrated on controlling my reaction. I reminded myself that even though I thought it was silly to be in trouble for something that seemed so insignificant, I still had the power to be in control of me. Suddenly, I was responding to my mother in a calm tone and simply explained why I had not done what she had asked me to do. Rather than conjure up some off-the-wall excuse that wouldn't have gotten me off the hook and probably landed me in even more trouble, I decided to just be honest. I even thought through my answer before I said it. What I found, as a result, was that my mother's reaction to me was different than it had been in the past when my response had been laced with attitude. Instead of one of my privileges being taken away, I was just asked once again to do what I was supposed to do in the first place. Amazing.

My first true experience with change, and it all began with me. It was then that I started to really understand that if I wanted something different, or if I wanted to be different, I was the one who had to change – not anyone else around me. From that moment on, when I found myself longing for something new or different I would step back and examine myself to figure out what I was *able* to change and then I would concentrate on *being* that change.

I would have another important experience with this concept when I was 16. One day it hit me that I wanted to do more with my life and wasn't satisfied with the idea of a typical job, like most of my friends. Fast food or retail just wasn't going to cut it for me, I decided. Even though it meant missing out on the whole summer between my junior and senior year of high school, I enrolled in beauty school to get my manicuring license. This left me with a total of two days of summer vacation, but I kept telling myself "If I want more out of my life, and myself, then I have to make a priority of the things that are important." I wanted a career, not just a "job" and the only way I was going to get there was to sacrifice a summer of fun and go to school instead.

The summer flew by and at the end I was a self-employed entrepreneur at just 17! I had made the choice to initiate the change I wanted, and was now on my way to a real career. When I returned to high school, I worked every day after school as well as each weekend. During the winter break, I worked full-time for the entire break but I didn't mind because I was making more money than I had ever thought possible. I was working for myself, essentially running my own business and I felt like I was light years beyond all of my friends. At that point, I also thought I knew everything I needed to know; I had found my career and no longer needed to worry about college. Then it hit me – why did I need to go back to high school after the winter break? I didn't just have a job, I had a career, and college sure wasn't in my long term plans so high school was starting to seem like a great big waste of time.

When school started again after the break, I wasn't there. After all, I already knew everything I needed to know about life, right? It wasn't until a few years later that I realized just how wrong I was and so very much more I still had to learn.

My life has never been one of stagnation; I am always learning or growing in some way, so I began to feel a bit unhappy and quite a bit unfulfilled. At 20 years old I was making only slightly more money than I had been making when I was 17. As I had done many times before I asked myself "Who is in charge of your life, Shar?" and I arrived at the same answer – I am; and I have to be the change I want. So, I sat down that day and did a little math. I knew that there was only so much money people were willing to pay to get their nails done. Even if I worked 12 hour days, there was a limit to just how much money I would be able to make.

Tip #4- Look at the big picture.
Sometimes it's smaller than you think.

Something had to change. Not only was I no longer learning, or growing, my income wasn't really going anywhere either. I had so many things I wanted to do in life – I wanted to travel, to experience a world beyond what I knew, to get involved with charities and to really make a difference. But how could I possibly do that sitting at my station for hours on end, making a decent living but certainly not enough to realize my dreams? I needed to figure out a way to get where I knew I was meant to be.

A few days later I was driving home from a long day of work and passed an Air Force Recruitment Center. Travel. Possibilities. Adventure. Suddenly, I'd found the opportunity I was looking for. I turned around and went inside the center to talk to a recruitment officer. As quickly as my hopes for a new future began to take shape, they were suddenly scattered in pieces around me. According to the recruiter, GEDs aren't accepted by the Air Force. Only a high school diploma will get you in the door. I left the building feeling as though a brick wall had fallen directly on my chest and saying to myself "Think beyond the 'now' before making big decisions that could drastically affect the rest of your life."

Almost immediately I enrolled in Adult Education classes. For several months, I took night classes and at the age of 20 finally received my high school diploma – and breathed a huge sigh of relief.

What this experience taught me was to seriously consider the choices you make and understand how they will affect the rest of your life. One of the exercises I would go through before making a potentially life-altering decision was to think about how I would feel sharing this choice with others. Even though it seemed like the answer to everything at the time, I never once felt proud about dropping out of high school and getting my GED. Every time someone asked if I had graduated I always told them yes and each time I heard the lie escape my lips, I felt ashamed. Not only because I wasn't being honest, but also because of the choice I'd made. These feelings, which always began deep inside my gut, should have been my first clue. Your gut is an excellent spokesperson for your true feelings, and mine was telling me that I needed to do something that would make me proud.

Change is inevitable – it's a side effect of life. After I received my diploma, I felt better about myself and about the direction I was headed. Suddenly it seemed as though new doors had been opened and my access to possibilities increased. Just as I was looking for the next step, it found me instead. I met a man, dated casually, then gradually reached a point where we decided not to see anyone else. By the time I was 21 we were engaged. Between them, my parents had been divorced nine times so it goes without saying that I had a pretty jaded view of marriage – but it seemed like the logical next step.

Even though we had been together for two years, there were still red flags that just wouldn't seem to go away. No one is perfect, I kept telling myself, and I was convinced that anything I didn't particularly like would change "after we got married." Deep inside I knew better, but for some reason I thought that walk down the aisle would result in a magical transformation and suddenly those red flags would be folded up and tucked away forever. Was I ever wrong.

When "real life" kicked in and when the proverbial honeymoon was over I couldn't escape the glaring issues. We disagreed on kids, money, health and lifestyle – pretty fundamental differences. I couldn't figure out how we ended up on such different pages and, more importantly, I couldn't figure out how I'd gotten myself into this situation to begin with. It didn't matter how hard I looked for the responsible party, the finger always pointed to me and one day I thought "You did this to yourself, Sharmen. You're the one that made the choice."

Now what? I had only been married for a year and a half and I already wanted out. In my mind, the marriage was over. He wanted kids right now; I wanted a career. At that point, I was working three jobs trying to get ahead which quickly became the source of much animosity in my marriage. In an attempt to stop some of the arguing, I quit two of my jobs and cut my hours back to part time on the one job I had left. Then one day I looked in the mirror and literally said out loud "What are you doing?!" Almost overnight I had turned into someone I didn't like, and definitely didn't want to be. I suggested counseling, which we tried for a while but in the end I went back to the only solution I knew. I filed for divorce.

Here I was again, faced with yet more change – change that I had chosen and a mess I had created. Yet, just as I had chosen to get into the situation, I was empowered with the ability to choose to get out. So, I packed my things and moved six hours away and decided to make a fresh start. I moved from Southern California to Northern California where my Dad lived. Both recently divorced, we saw this as an opportunity to have a father/daughter relationship that just wasn't possible when I was a young girl. Growing up, my Dad lived about six hours from us which meant my time with him was limited to only a couple visits a year, if we were that lucky. As a result I always felt as though I missed out on being "Daddy's girl" so when the chance to finally know my father became a reality, I was ecstatic.

Yet again, I found myself face to face with change. When a tempting offer from a telephone company came my way, I sat down and reevaluated my life. Again. I took a good hard look at each area of my life that I wasn't happy with and that I wanted to change – keeping in mind that any change had to begin with me. I was an Administrative Assistant at the time and truly did enjoy the work. I was learning a lot, taking computer classes and was becoming trained in other office management skills. I had never worked in Corporate America and was finding out just how much I didn't know and how much I still had to learn, especially about the telecommunications industry. Suddenly I no longer felt stagnant.

A few short months later I moved up from temp to permanent employee. My computer skills had become much stronger and I was still constantly learning and refining my skills. One year later I was up for a promotion. I finally saw a window of opportunity opening to achieve my goals – a window, unfortunately, that was quickly shut. Not only did the company hire someone from the outside the company, but then I was expected to train her! What? Are you kidding me? I was good enough to train someone to do the job but not quite good enough to do it myself?

At that point, I chose to take a few humble steps back from the situation and take a deep, but painful, breath. I thought back to what I might have done that could have taken me out of the running for the promotion and opened it up to an outsider. But I struggled to come up with even one single misstep on my part. I recalled nights where I hadn't slept, not even for 10 minutes, going above and beyond what was even expected or required of me – giving more than 100% in everything that I did. There had been mention of my lack of a college degree, but surely that couldn't have overshadowed the work I had done and how I had proven myself to be a dedicated and hardworking employee. Yet, the comments about my lack of a formal education just wouldn't stay in the back of my mind. No matter what, they always seemed to creep back in until I was forced to come to grips with what I knew was true, but had hoped so intently would prove to be false.

Suddenly it became abundantly clear that my decision to end my education after high school would always hold me back. First, it was my lack of a high school diploma that caused one opportunity to pass me by. Was I just going to sit back and allow the same to happen because I had not gone to college?

No, I wasn't. The very next day I went to the community college in my city and enrolled in classes. This was the first, and monumental, step toward making a tremendous change in my life – a change that would prove to be nearly unending. At the age of 24, when most young adults were graduating from or finished with college, I was just starting my journey. The important realization at the forefront of my mind, however, was that it was not too late.

Tip #5- Change is inevitable

The internal struggle I faced was my inability to justify in my mind just exactly what I was doing. I knew it wasn't a bad thing that I was pursuing my degree; I was doing what I had always valued – learning, growing and bettering myself. Yet what I failed to recognize was why it mattered so much to anyone else. At that stage in my career I had encountered numerous people with college degrees, some of them from "designer" schools with hefty price tags offering even heftier pedigrees. But they were, for all intents and purposes, pretty average people. While I was never one to walk around with an over-inflated ego, I couldn't shake the feeling that my life and professional experience had taught me so much more than what most people learned sitting in a classroom or lecture hall for four years. Surely the energy and time I had expended gaining life experience, and learning how to operate successfully in the professional world had to be worth something, right?

While I struggled internally with these seemingly contradictory ideals, I decided that I had to heed the age-old adage which instructs us to fight only those battles which we can win. And I did just that. It wasn't as though I was doing something that I did not want to do, or that I disagreed with. Earning my college degree was always part of my long term plan, I had just always expected it to be done on my terms, when I was ready, and when I felt it was necessary – not when someone else set those requirements for me. Rather than allow any feelings of resentment overshadow my overall goal, I took the attitude that I was doing this entirely for myself and for the reasons I had always anticipated. So the timeline was pushed up a bit, so what, in the end it would benefit me and push me even further ahead than where I already was.

Eventually, I quit my job and accepted a position with another company in the same role. I gave it my best shot at the phone company, but in the end the fact that I had been passed up for the promotion got the best of me. Had I been offered the job, which I felt I had worked for and earned, I would have stayed and hopefully progressed within the company. Yet, if my life has taught me anything it's that every single thing happens for a reason. Even when it feels as though your world is crashing around you, somehow, someway, in the end there is good to be found. My new job came with a higher salary, a better office, a more impressive title and support like nothing I had experienced at any stage in my career. When I stop and think back to that time it is so crystal clear to me that the universe was sending me a message. While the delivery could have used some improvement, it was telling me that I was capable of so much more than what I was doing and that I was ultimately destined for bigger and better.

Once again, change was upon me. Though it was wrapped in a pretty dreary package, it presented new and exciting opportunities. As with most people and most jobs, things begin to lose their luster. Yet again, I found myself repeating the phrase that had carried me to where I currently was, "If you want your situation to change, you have to be the change." Right then, I found a pen and paper and began to make a list of all the things I didn't like in my life in one column, and then in a second column I wrote down what I would like to see replace each of those things. For one, I was surrounded by people who were not any smarter than me and certainly did not work harder than I did. Yet, for some reason, they were making thousands and thousands of dollars more than I was. I knew I could do their jobs.

Shortly thereafter, I began a new career in sales in the mortgage business. In just a few years I was making more than a million dollars a year. Not only that, I was helping others and giving back by supporting charities and causes I believed in. When I took the time to stop and think back to the many steps in my journey to success, it was amazing how many times I could recall feeling as though I was at the end of my rope. The times when it seemed as though nothing could get worse, and I would never get past some negative event or occurrence, it always turned around and evolved into being the best thing that had ever happened to me. I was perfectly happy with my job as a secretary, or administrative assistant, and probably would not have left the company if I'd received the promotion I so wanted at the time. I concentrated all of the disappointment I felt in not being offered the job into the positive energy required to make a change – a change that would prove to have an extraordinary impact on the rest of my life.

Do you find yourself thinking and feeling some of the very things I've described about my life? Chances are if you have picked up this book you do. It is much easier to continue on the same old path in life, even if it's an unhappy one. Change is hard. Identifying what you want to change is even harder. But, if you are up for the challenge I am here to show you how to tackle both.

The first thing you need to do is ask yourself the tough questions. You know you don't like your life, but do you know why? Knowing the why is the first step to making that change. Try it now. Take out a piece of paper and write down what you don't like about your life. Don't hold anything back even though at first you will feel like you are oozing with negativity. That's okay. The only way to figure out what you want to change is to identify the aspects of your life that you don't like.

Remember this isn't about being nice or polite or proper. This is about using words with power in order to force yourself to do something about your life. In fact, sometimes it's nice to just get all the crap out of our system and start over with a clean slate. Think of it as a mental cleanse. You are getting all the toxins and impurities out of your mind so you can replace them with incredible and extraordinary things.

For this exercise and the others throughout this book it is important to write your answers out, not just think about them – write down whatever comes to mind. Permanently putting the answers on paper gives them a power that simply thinking about them cannot.

Tip #6- Flush out the negative

Exercise 1.1

1. Write down the parts of your life you are unhappy, frustrated and simply not satisfied with. All the things you find yourself complaining about every day. Don't be afraid. Don't hold anything back. Write down all the aspects of your life you don't like or downright hate.

How did that feel? I still do this exercise pretty often and I always feel so much lighter and freer after I have done it. It is a great way to purge your system of the weeks, months or possibly even years of garbage that you and others have been putting into your head.

What did you come up with? Do you live paycheck to paycheck, have a job that you hate or no job at all? Do you rent an apartment that you don't like? Is your relationship not what you want it to be? Well, I've been there. I had a job that was okay, an apartment that was just average and life that was nothing special. If you find yourself here or somewhere similar day in and day out, then you probably already know the parts of your life you want to change. Yet, it's great to put them on paper because this is what makes them real and truly brings them to life. At least now you can do something about them. I have done this exercise with many people and I've done it myself many times. One day I wrote down all the things I wasn't happy with. Then I took a moment to look over my list and wrote a new list of all the things that were possible in place of the negative. That will be your next exercise.

Tip #7- Turn your don't wants into do wants

<u>Exercise 1.2</u>

1. Get out another piece of paper. On the top left write HAVE. On the top right write WANT.
2. Rewrite everything that you said you didn't like about your life under the HAVE column.
3. On the right, under the WANT column, write what you want in its place. If you don't know, just write the polar opposite.

If you wrote that you hate your job, write down your dream job. If you don't like how much you weigh, write down how much you want to weigh. If you don't like where you live, write down where you would love to live. Go down your entire list of don't likes or don't wants and write what you do like and want.

The most important thing here is to throw all reason, rational and reality out the window. This is not a reality job it is your dream job. Or, perhaps you are looking for the man or woman of your dreams. That's okay too. Write down all of the qualities you want that person to have. What would he/she look like? What would you do together? Where would you go together? What goals would he/she have? What would your goals be together?

Don't worry about how you are going to get these things. Don't ask if it even exists. We will deal with that later. Just take this opportunity to find out for yourself what you really want. Have fun with it. Write down all the thoughts and ideas you have for your perfect job, spouse, home, car, education, etc.

When I was 20 I did this very exercise. I found out a lot of things about myself. I knew I wanted a different job. One that allowed me all the things I never had growing up. I wanted a bit of freedom and flexibility. And, I didn't want to be stuck in an office. Knowing what I wanted was only half the battle. Admitting what I needed to do to get there was another thing. The hardest pill for me to swallow was realizing that in order to accomplish this dream of a better life I was going to have to get my high school diploma, not just my GED.

Dropping out of high school only a few months before graduation was a product of my upbringing. I already had a job making more money than my friends were. On top of that no one in my family had gone to college. Therefore, I didn't see why I needed to be there. Back then I saw my upbringing and position in life as a roadblock. A little soul searching later in life made me realize that these roadblocks were merely stepping stones. I realized that my life was full of endless opportunities. I was not doomed to repeat my parent's life. You need to believe the universe is full of endless opportunities because it is. There are no limits! Boundaries are only stepping stones. The only limits on what you can be, do or have are the ones that you create in your own head.

The difference between successful people and unsuccessful people is that successful people see the possibilities where others see the roadblocks. Do you think that there are possibilities everywhere? If you believe that there are no possibilities beyond what you already are, do or have, then you are right. Better things are not possible for you. Something more, something else, something different is always possible. But, first you must believe it. If you dropped out of high school you can always go back and finish. I did. If you have your bachelor's degree, go get your master's. If you already have your master's, go get your doctorate. If you have your doctorate, you can get another one. If you make a million go make two or ten or a billion. You should always be learning, doing, growing, and achieving.

Tip #8- The possibilities are endless.

Think about all the extraordinary things, all the modern conveniences that we are fortunate to have. Think about the first television or automobile. What about the internet? Once upon a time there was no such thing. These are things that someone thought was possible and then made a reality. Now it's your turn. What is possible for you?

Tip #9- Identify all the possibilities

Exercise 1.3

1. Write down all the things you think are possible. Don't stop at answering these questions. If more is possible for you then write it down.
2. What is the highest possible income you can imagine making?
3. How much is it possible for you to have in the bank?
4. How much real estate can you own?
5. What is the most you can imagine spending on a car?
6. What is the highest level of education you think is possible for you to achieve?
7. Where is it possible for you to go on vacation?
8. How many vacations is it possible for you to take a year?
9. What is the smallest clothing size you can imagine fitting into?
10. What is your ideal weight?
11. What characteristics would your perfect life partner have?
12. What else is possible for you?

Look over your answers. What do you see? Are you finally seeing life as limitless with infinite possibilities? I certainly hope so.

LESSONS LEARNED

*   Don't be afraid to ask yourself the tough questions and really hear the answers.
*   Your current position in life is not a roadblock only a stepping-stone.
*   Life is full of endless possibilities.
*   Work on one goal at a time.

Chapter 2:
What Makes You Tick?

Sometimes the things we want in life change. Something you love today, may not be what you love a year or two, or even ten years later. Sometimes we let life get in the way and forget the things that are really important to us. We forget the things that light us up. Once again this is about being that change. It's making the choice to not get distracted and let life get in the way. No matter how you slice it, no matter how much we rationalize what we do and why we do it, in the end we are making a choice.

"What makes me tick? What do I absolutely love to do? In a perfect world, where I could describe the exact life I want, what would it look like?" Ask yourself this: If I could do anything I wanted, had all the money and resources I needed, and was guaranteed to succeed, what would I want to be, do or have?

For me it's writing and speaking. Although, I forgot about that for a long time. When I was a kid I would write silly little stories. Sometimes they made no sense at all. But it was a great outlet and something I did any time I got the chance. How did I forget that? When things weren't going right in my life I would write in my journal. When things went great in my life I wrote in my journal. When I wanted to really tell someone how I felt, I would write to them. When I was feeling creative I would write.

Then there was speaking. Even at 12 years old in the seventh grade when I had to give a speech about myself, I first wrote out what I wanted to say then I couldn't wait to stand up in front of my classmates and give my speech. I loved to do verbal book reports. I had so much fun even while my friends and other classmates hated it. Anything to do with writing and speaking, I absolutely loved.

Yet somehow pursuing a job in writing or speaking didn't occur to me at the time. So I ended up doing other things. Manicuring, Phlebotomy, Secretary, Sales. They all served their purpose for the time being but none of them were my passion.

When I was in the mortgage business I was doing a job that I liked and was good at but it was by no means my passion. It didn't light my fire. I didn't get up in the morning excited because I got to go sell mortgages. After selling mortgages for a few years I didn't really even enjoy it any more. The problem was I had no idea what else I could do. What else would I want to do? I was one of those people that didn't know what I was passionate about.

I remember thinking one day about six years into the mortgage business "I can't do this job for much longer. I've been working my tail off for years, I'm exhausted and I'm tired of being at my clients beck and call just so they can send their loan to another lender for a fraction of a reduced rate. But what would I do if I weren't doing this?" The big dark question mark loomed over my head for the next few months.

One day my boss asked me to fill in at a speaking event she could not attend and I agreed. I had spoken many times before but only in front of small groups of about 10 or 20. There were supposed to be close to 100 people at this event. I figured what the heck? What's a few more people? The day came, I stood at the podium and gave my five minute speech and took my seat for the Q & A session. I felt elated. I couldn't remember the last time I felt that kind of a rush. Later, I had several of my colleagues and members of the audience say, "Wow, Shar. You were by far the best panelist. You are a really good speaker."

For months I couldn't stop thinking about that day and the feeling that I had. Where did this come from? I swear I had felt it before, but for the life of me I couldn't remember when. So, I went back to what I knew had worked for me in the past. Anytime I was confused or looking for direction, I would write. I grabbed a journal and started writing down questions. "When have I felt this way before? How many times have I felt this way?" I let the questions flow. I have to be honest. I was a little disappointed. Absolutely no answers came to mind. I went to sleep with those questions still floating around in my head.

Tip #10- Getting a good answer, starts with asking a good question.

I woke up in the middle of the night with a flood of thoughts. All of a sudden I remembered when I had felt that same rush. When I was in the seventh grade I had to stand in front of my class and give a "me speech." A few years later, in my freshman English class, I had to do an oral book report on *The Lion, the Witch and the Wardrobe*. Then sophomore year there was another oral book report on *My Fair Lady*. I remembered other kids telling me "You are amazing. How do you do it? Everyone but you hates to do these speeches, but you seem to love it." That same year I remember being at an assembly where a speaker addressed the whole school. There were big white screens on the stage that flashed images of the speaker as he was talking. Then there was loud, awesome, motivating music in the background. I was mesmerized. I remembered thinking "I wish that were me. I would love to do that. I can see myself doing that." I remember asking my school counselor, "How do I get that kind of job? What is that job called?" To this day I have no memory of the answer.

It was then that I had the "ah-ha". I realized what my passion was. From that point forward, I seized every opportunity to speak.

I still had my sales job, but I enjoyed it less and less each day. I had on what's known as the golden handcuffs. I was making in the high six, sometimes seven, figures a year, and didn't know how to leave what

I was doing to do something I had a complete and total passion for. I did know that every time I was speaking, I felt alive. From that point forward I made sure I was speaking in front of at least a few people on a regular basis and if for some reason I couldn't I was writing something I wanted to speak about, every day.

Two years later I was at a seminar hosted by my company for its customers. After the seminar I put together a proposal with the content I wanted to speak about then went to the person in charge and said, "There are six men on that platform. Why are there no women?" He told me they were looking for a woman but they hadn't found the right one yet. So I told him, "I would like to be the woman speaker," and gave him my proposal. He said, "Okay, we'll give you a shot at the next seminar. It's in two weeks." I was thrilled.

When I was told they were expecting two thousand people at that seminar I remember thinking, "Oh my God, what have I gotten myself into?" The day of the event I had a feeling of exhilaration combined with fear. I asked myself, "What's the worst that can happen? I could fail miserably, fall flat on my face, or worse throw up right there on stage." I decided if any of those happened then I would know for sure that big time public speaking wasn't for me.

Obviously, none of the above happened. I was standing in the back of a two thousand person audience and when I heard my introduction and my name, I started walking towards the stage. I walked up three stairs, stood on the stage and looked out to the audience. An audience so large, I couldn't see to the back of the room. I was sure everyone could hear my heart beating through my chest. Then I started to speak. My heart rate slowed down, my shoulders relaxed and I felt like I was doing what I was born to do. I had never felt so alive in all my life. I remember thinking, "This is such a rush. I could do this for the rest of my life." And that was it. I knew what I needed to do.

That year I made just under a million. That year was also when I started developing a plan to leave my job in sales and pursue my true passion – speaking. I knew I could do more than I was doing. I knew

I had a message that could help others. I had been told many times by many people that I was an inspiration. I knew I had something in me that made me want to share my story to empower others to be, do and have everything they want.

I started accepting paid speaking engagements on the weekends. I began an outline for a book and grew to live out my passion. About a year later, I quit the job that was making me millions. It was not an easy decision, and I got a great deal of criticism from those I worked with. In fact, I received so much criticism there were some moments I found myself rethinking my decision. However, deep down inside, I knew I didn't love my job. I knew I would burn out because I worked too hard and too long doing something I didn't love. Most of the time, I didn't even like it anymore. Ultimately, I decided that if I was going to spend hours and hours a day working at anything, I wanted it to be at something for which I had passion.

I can tell you from experience that it doesn't matter how much money you make if you don't enjoy what you're doing. And, there is no better feeling than waking up every day to something about which you are passionate. I wish everyone in the world could feel this way because it is better than anything else I have ever experienced.

Tip #11- Getting paid to do what you love... now that's living!

So, what makes you tick? What drives you? What gives you that rush? What is your purpose in life? What is your calling? What is your passion? Everyone is passionate about something. Ask a professional athlete, doctor, fireman, teacher, pilot, or policeman. Most of the time, they knew since they were children what they wanted to be when they grew up. But, what if you don't know? I had several coaching clients that had no idea what they were passionate about. I'd ask them what they would do if they could choose their job out of a catalog of infinite possibilities. More times than not the answer was "I don't know." There is nothing wrong with not knowing.

Ask yourself now, "What am I passionate about?" If nothing comes to mind that's ok. Just relax and take a deep breath. Here are a few questions that can help you find the answers. Get out a journal and write them down. Just thinking about the answers won't cut it. In order to really have a breakthrough and make a difference, you must write them down.

Tip #12- Find your passion!

Exercise 2.1

Question 1. If you died tomorrow, what would you regret having not done?

Question 2. If you only had one week left to live, what would you make sure you do?

Question 3. What do you feel you were put on this Earth to do?

Question 4. Do you have something that you deeply care about?

Question 5. Do you find yourself consistently thinking about something or having a recurring thought, dream, or vision?

Question 6. Name five things you are really good at?

Question 9. Ask five people what they think you are good at?

Question 10. If you had a week all to yourself with no responsibilities how would you spend it?

Question 11. Name five things you enjoy doing?

Question 12. Name one thing you do that makes hours go by in what feels like minutes.

Question 13. What do you find yourself reading, listening to or watching on television or what movies do you find interesting?

Question 14. Pay attention to the things you find yourself saying, "I wish" to. "I wish I could do that. If only I had the time, money, etc."

Question 15.   Do you secretly know what you are passionate about but are also secretly afraid how others, be it friends, family, bosses, colleagues, etc. will judge you?

Question 16.   If there were a recipe for success, a guaranteed plan to ensure you would not fail, what would you do?

Question 17.   Name a time when you felt on top of the world and you felt as if you were unstoppable. What were you doing?

Look over your answers. Most likely there are some common threads. Do the same or similar answers come up more than once? Did something someone said you were good at get you to thinking? Sometimes there are things we take for granted, that other people can see. Chances are you have some ideas on things you haven't thought about in years.

My Dad once said, "I don't feel passionate about anything. I can't think of anything that gets me excited. Things I do or have done, just don't light me up." I remembered things that he was good at and thoroughly enjoyed. I responded with, "Are you kidding me? What about theater? You used to love to do local theater or anything that had you on stage acting. Or, how about motorcycles? No matter how many motorcycle accidents you get into you insist on owning and riding a bike. You are willing to risk your life to ride a motorcycle. If that's not passion I don't know what is!"

He responded with, "I can't believe you would mention motorcycles. You hate motorcycles." He was absolutely correct. I do not like motorcycles at all. He had been in three accidents and each one was worse than the last. My point here is very, very important and it's your next tip.

Tip #13- It doesn't matter what anyone else's opinion or judgment is about your passion. It is still *your* passion.

When I was making over seven figures a year and would complain about my life, that I wasn't happy for this reason or that, people said I was insane. I was told I was selfish and self absorbed because I wanted more than what I had. Quite frankly that was their story and their problem, not mine. I highly doubt that Oprah Winfrey, Donald Trump, Bill Gates, or Warren Buffett would say or think that my goals were selfish or self absorbed. You live your life, no one else does. So you choose what you want.

Tip #14- Get clear about what you want

Exercise 2.2

1. Write down what your passions are.
2. What are the costs of not following your passion?
3. What are the obstacles you expect to face if you follow your passion?
4. What do you lose if you don't follow your passion?
5. What do you gain by finding and following your passion?
6. Are you committed to making that passion happen?

Right now I hope you are on the path to knowing your passion. Then next step is to incorporate your passion into your life. Can you think of a better way to begin or end every single day than by indulging in your passion? No matter what makes you tick you should incorporate it into your life in some way. Even better, be it, do it, or have it every day. Do you love music? Then wake up each and every day to your favorite music. If your happiest moment is starting the day with a cup of coffee sitting quietly by yourself while looking out the window, then do it. If reading is your passion, make a commitment to read a little bit every day. If you love to write, or learn, or talk, or work out, or sing, or whatever, do it. Do it at a minimum of once a week.

Once upon a time, I didn't know what I loved or wanted to do. I just kind of did whatever came at me. I had a J-O-B. It was what I did eight hours a day, five days a week, 52 weeks a year. With the amount of time we all spend at our J-O-B, I believe it should be something that we love, something that makes us tick. I forgot that for about 20 years. I was fortunate enough to find it again. I discovered as a kid that I loved to speak in front of people and even though I lost sight of my passion for many years, I found it again. That is my wish for you. Find what makes you tick, then find a way to do it!

Are you thinking, "Yeah, right sister, it just ain't that simple. Tell me how to incorporate my passion into my life!" I can't do it for you. I can only give you the tools and information for you to take action on and do something with. Having said that, I can give you some steps to get you thinking in the right direction. But, you have to do the work and find what works for you. Again, you must write your answers down. Just thinking about them and having them roll around in your head is not powerful enough to get you to take action. When it is just an idea or a thought scrambling in your head, it's very easy to forget. Writing things down makes them real and tangible and gives you the template to work with. Do the exercise below and you will be on your way to incorporating your passion into your life.

Tip #15- Make time for your passion.

Exercise 2.3

1. How often do I want to do _____ (name your passion)?
2. When is the best time for me to do _____ _____? (weekends, weekdays, nights, mornings, afternoon, lunchtime, etc)
3. Write it on your calendar. Don't just put it in your PDA, BlackBerry or other electronic device. The problem with

electronic calendars is that you don't see it in front of you all the time. You only see it when the reminder you set pops up. I suggest buying a regular 12 month calendar to put in the bathroom or kitchen. Somewhere that you will see it at least once a day.

4. Rearrange your schedule so this will become a regular routine thing you do and are highly unlikely to have something else come up.

5. Schedule it on the calendar regularly until it becomes a habit. After it becomes a habit, keep writing it on the calendar to keep yourself honest!

6. Get an accountability partner or coach. Find someone you can count on to check in with regularly to make sure you are staying on track.

7. Follow through. DO IT! You have already set the stage now you just have to show up.

At this point you have an idea of what you are passionate about and have a plan to incorporate it into your life. What's next? Would you like to make money doing your passion? I believe there is nothing better in the world than making money at something you love to do. However, the big question gets to be, "How do I do it?"

I know a woman who loved to belly dance. She took a class in her late teens and fell in love with it. She later got a second job as a secretary just so she could afford to do her hobby. One day she thought, "If I love dancing and can't wait everyday to do it and am paying someone else to let me do it, why don't I make dancing my job?" She then quit her day job and became a professional belly dancer, traveling the world, performing her passion. Now she is getting paid to do what she loves.

Her name is Sandra and she didn't stop there. After traveling the world dancing and loving it, she thought "What happens when I'm not dancing? I don't get paid." After putting together a plan, she came up with a way to get paid even when she wasn't working. She rented a studio where she could teach others to dance, but also hired other dancers to teach as well. That way if she wanted a day off, went on vacation, or was off in some foreign land performing, the other instructors would still be teaching while she was gone, ultimately making money even though she wasn't doing the work.

I think you are probably getting the picture. However, this story gets even better. Sandra, being clearly talented and brilliant, decided to take it a step further. She learned about something called Permanent Residual Income. In one sentence, Permanent Residual Income can be described as: do the work once and keep getting paid.

Tip #16- Find a way to do the work once and keep getting paid.

Owning your own business is great, but it does come with a great deal of risk. There are expenses that go along with owning that business. There are employee salaries to pay, insurance, rent or mortgage on the space, equipment, utilities, and so on. So how can you create Permanent Residual Income with little to no residual expenses? Remember, do the work once and keep getting paid. Sandra knew everything there was to know about belly dancing. She also loved murder mystery books. How could she combine the two? How about write a belly dancing murder mystery. And that is exactly what Sandra did.

On March 26, 2008 *The African Belly Dance* by Sandra Catena was released. Now every day Sandra wakes up she has money in the bank that wasn't there the night before. People go to her website and buy her book. When Sandra is performing somewhere people buy her book. When she is at her studio, people buy her book. No matter what Sandra is doing, her book is selling. She now makes Permanent Residual Income because she found her passion, did her passion every day, and found a way to make money doing it.

I love to read. I love to write, and speak and empower others. That's all fine and dandy, but how do you make money doing that? I found a way to pretty much combine all my passions, do the work once and make money doing it. I wrote a book giving people the tools to create the life they want. Then I started doing keynotes, seminars and workshops on the topics covered in the book. After the book, came the audio book, after the audio book, came the video, after the video, came the workbook, after the workbook came all of them together in a home study program. One idea led to another and another. The beautiful thing is, I only had to do the work once and the products continue to sell, creating residual income.

In doing research to write this book, I discovered countless people who have found a way to make money doing what they love and only had to do the work once. One woman I interviewed enjoyed reading. She learned how to proofread and started proofreading books for publishing houses before they went into publication. Being an actress, she was on the road a lot, but she was able to bring her work with her. And by work I mean, she would read books. Soon she started teaching others how to proofread. Then her entrepreneurial mind kicked in. Instead of teaching proofreading to people one by one, she decided to write a book training people how to get paid to proofread.

She then got a website and made the introduction of the book available for free in exchange for an email address. If the reader liked the introduction, they could download the entire book for $24.95. The best part about this is that there was no overhead. Since it was an eBook she didn't have to produce a physical product. Eventually she got a call from the people who publish the "For Dummies" book series. They told her they were looking to do a book titled *Copyediting and Proofreading for Dummies* and in their search for an author found that she dominated the market. Next thing she knew *Copyediting and Proofreading for Dummies* by Suzanne Gilad was published and in every bookstore in America.

How about exercise? Do you work out? Do you have some technique that works amazingly well? Do you do something different that no one else does? I know a man who was a personal trainer. He made a video with step-by-step instructions on how to perform his special exercises and made it available for purchase both on DVD and download. Again, no matter where he is or what he is doing, money flows into his account because people buy his video on his website even when he's sleeping.

Ever hear of Bill Phillips? The author of *Body For Life, Eating for Life* and former CEO of EAS. Bill started his entrepreneurial career writing a newsletter for bodybuilders about how to use anabolic steroids. This was at a time when they were not illegal. Since then he wrote the book *Body For Life*. Which, by the way, has sold over three million copies and was on the *New York Times* bestseller list for more than three years. He had a passion, he was an expert and found a way to make money doing it.

There are many ways to make money doing your passion. Write a newsletter, pamphlet or book. Record an audio instruction guide, or video. Teach others how to do it and work out an agreement for a referral fee or percent of profits. Do you know how to get red wine stains out of anything? Write an article on it and sell it on your website. Do you run a daycare? Write a book on how to open your own daycare.

Maybe what you're good at is a little on the risqué side. Did you know there is a book called *Tickle His Pickle*? A woman found a way to make money by being a "pleasure coach" and wrote a book on how to pleasure a man's penis. There is a book that teaches how to pole dance. If someone can find a way to make money doing that, you can find a way to make money doing just about anything!

By now I hope your creative juices are flowing. There are a myriad of ways you can make money doing what you love. There is no better way to spend the day than doing something you love and getting paid for it.

Now for your last passion exercise. Again, don't just think, write.

Tip #17- Make money at your passion!

Exercise 2.4

1. Write down the passion you want to focus on?
2. Write down at least five ways you can make money doing it?

3. How much time do you want to dedicate to making money doing your passion?

4. How much money do you want to make per week doing your passion?

5. Do some research to see if anyone else is doing it. If someone else is, can you improve on it and do it better or differently?

6. Write down the things you need to do to get the ball rolling on your money making machine.

7. Take action and do it!

So that's it. You should now know what you are passionate about, how to incorporate that passion into your life and how to make money doing it if you want to.

LESSONS LEARNED

1. The importance of having passion
2. How to find your passion
3. How to incorporate your passion into your life
4. How to make money at your passion

Chapter 3:
Make Your Tick Talk

It was truly liberating when I found my passion. I hope finding yours has the same effect on you. Knowing what you are passionate about in and of itself is wonderful, especially if you had forgotten what it was! But what do you do with it now?

Now you get to give your passion a voice – make what makes you tick, talk. I'm talking about setting your goals. If you don't know what you want you will get whatever comes at you. And you will likely wonder "how did I get this?" The reason you got what you got is because you didn't do anything to get what you wanted. Just like going on vacation, if you don't know where you want to go you will end up someplace else.

I find goal setting to be fun. I love when I'm aspiring to accomplish something new. I remember when I was in junior high school and was the majorette for the school band. Yes being in "band" was so not cool in those days, but I loved twirling the baton. I had loved it since I was a little kid. Looking back, this was one of my first experiences with goal setting.

We were going to a competition and I just knew I had a shot at first place. It wasn't going to be easy but I knew I could do it. My goal: the first place trophy. I had to beef up my routine, add some elements that were more difficult and perform better than I had ever performed before which meant I would have to start working with a coach. The only problem was I was too young to get a job and I didn't have a way to pay for lessons. Yet, even at 13 years old I had a goal and I was going to make that goal happen. Eventually, I found a coach that needed an assistant, so we bartered. I helped her out at her practices and she gave me lessons in return. This is the first time I can remember setting a goal for something I wanted and made it happen. My hard work and dedication paid off because in the end I did take first place.

As I got older, that moment constantly reminded me of how important it was to be working towards something. I know I feel somewhat "blah" when I'm not focused on accomplishing anything. That's why I am always setting goals, little or big, just so I am always on the ball working to improve myself in some way.

Tip #18- The world does not stand still, why should you?

Obviously, as we get older our goals change. At one point in my life I was setting goals to win a gold medal or pass a test. Now my goals are things like speaking for a 25,000 person crowd or a Fortune 50 company. Or even, buy a house, make a million, get married, or change the world. I'm sure you know what I mean.

After high school, I really started setting big, important goals, things that could change my life. I had just moved from Southern California to Northern California and was searching for a new career. No more manicuring for me. What was I going to do now? I wanted something that wasn't limited, something that had growth potential. Next stop, vocational school.

I had never used a computer in my life at that point and if I was going to do something worthwhile I needed to learn. At the time I also couldn't type. It just wasn't something I needed as a manicurist so I never learned how.

I enrolled in an adult education school where I started taking typing and the basic classes learning computer software for the office.

I wanted to get it done as fast as possible so I took the next four weeks and crammed in as many classes as I could. Word, Excel, Office Assistant, Typing, and a few others. Taking those classes gave me what I needed to get a job with a temp agency and shortly thereafter helped me get the job at MCI. After I was passed up for the promotion and made the choice to leave, a friend told me about a company that was looking for an assistant to the VP of Operations. I applied immediately. Meanwhile, I did some research on the company and asked my friend what she knew about the person I would potentially be working for. Three weeks later I gave my notice at the phone company and was the new Executive Assistant to the VP of Operations.

Goals don't just happen overnight. And let me tell you, patience is not one of my best qualities. I had to remind myself many times that Rome wasn't built in a day and great things take time. Keeping that in mind I continued to set my goals so I at least knew what I was working towards.

I have learned over the years that there are things you can do to help make your goals read better so they are stronger and more likely to happen. Refer back to Exercise 1.2. The one where you named all the things you hate about your life and listed what you wanted instead.

Tip #19- Set a goal!

Exercise 3.1

1. Go through your entire list and turn your wants into goal statements.
2. Write down the one goal you want to start working towards today. Once you have reached that goal you can come back to the rest. It's best not to overwhelm yourself. One at a time is manageable.

There is a little trick to setting goals. There are two tools to use and apply to really lock them in and ensure your success. I have found that if you state the goal in the positive you get a better feeling about it. Things like "I am a 115 pound, lean, size four woman" worked so much better for me than "I want to lose ten pounds." The reason it worked so much better is because I was stating it in the positive. Which, in turn, makes it feel real and gives your goals life.

The second key factor I found in setting goals to give them that extra "oomph" is stating the goal in the present tense. Again, if you are looking to lose ten pounds writing your goal as "I am going to lose ten pounds" is not as effective as stating it as if you already have what you want. First and foremost, *going to* doesn't imply that you *are* doing it. Rather, it suggests that you are not doing it now, but are going to, soon. Also, when you say lose, it sounds as though you are taking something away. Think about some of the phrases that have the term lose in it. Do they make you feel good, or bad? *Loser. I'm going to lose my mind. We lost the game. I lost my keys.* Do any of these have any positive connotations to them? I don't think so. Therefore, if you currently weigh 150 pounds but want to weigh 140 pounds say, "I feel great at my happy weight of 140 pounds." Or, say you are going to start exercising and cut out sugary foods from your daily eating habits. The positive, present way to say it is, "I am healthy and fit. I exercise four days a week and only eat healthy, nutritionally sound foods. I feel better than I have ever felt before."

Maybe you have a date by which you want to achieve your goal. Write it as if it has already happened. If it's April 10 and you want to weigh 140 pounds by June 1, you should write, "It is June 1 and I am happy and proud to be at my goal weight of 140 pounds. I look and feel amazing."

You can also use this technique for money. If you currently make $50,000 a year and want to make $100,000 write, "I am making a six figure income doing what I love." Or using the date method, "It is December 31 and I made over six figures this year, I am debt free and have the lifestyle I've always wanted." You can do this for anything on your list. "I am with the partner of my dreams. He/she is my perfect match and we have an extraordinary relationship." "I am ecstatic! I have the best job in the world. I love what I do and I get paid seven figures to do it!" "I am a stay at home mom, I get to watch every moment of my child's life and I make six figures by following my passion part-time while my child naps." Do you get the picture? The list goes on and on. You can create anything you want when you start by setting your goals.

Just remember those two things when setting your goals, positive and present. Do, act and feel as if you have it now and you will!

Tip #20- Put one goal in writing!

Exercise 3.2

1. Write your one goal in the positive and in the present tense. Make sure there are no "nos", "don'ts", "wills", or "wants". Remember only one goal at a time. Once you have achieved that goal you can move on to more.

For me, my goal looked like this: "I have my actual high school diploma, not just my GED. I am a high school graduate." I looked at that goal every day and I went out and did it.

Once I had my high school diploma I knew it was time to tackle the next phase of my life transformation. I started making more goal statements. The next one was about my job. I wanted a job that would allow me the lifestyle I knew was possible. At the time I was working as an executive assistant to the VP of Operations who worked closely with the VP of Sales. I had heard that even the worst sales people were making $10,000 a month, some made even more than that. I wanted what they had. But, I was born and raised in a small city where people didn't make big money and didn't do big business. Big things were not in my scope of what was possible. It would have been easy to go on thinking that way, but I was aware of some very important realities.

These people making all that money weren't any smarter than me and they certainly weren't working any harder. So I wrote my goal statement: "I make $10,000 or more per month. I have freedom and flexibility in my job. I am doing my own thing with a supportive boss that leaves me alone and lets me get my work done." A few months later I found a sales job and was on my way.

This was the first time I felt as though I had chosen my life. I was setting goals for myself and getting what I wanted. I set a goal to get my high school diploma and I did it. I had a goal for the job I wanted and the next thing I knew I had that job. I started to write goals for everything I wanted to accomplish that year. I wanted to make $100,000. I wanted to drive a BMW. I wanted to buy my first pair of really nice, expensive shoes. I wanted freedom and flexibility and a job I liked. That year I made just under a hundred thousand dollars, got the new car and had the flexibility and freedom to do my job without a boss nagging at me or being chained to a desk. But, how did I do it? Yes, it started with setting the goal. But it certainly didn't end there.

LESSONS LEARNED

1. Write out goal statements in the positive and present.
2. Work on one goal at a time.

Chapter 4:
Take Your Talk for a Walk

Antoine de Saint-Exupery once said that "a goal without a plan is just a wish." Really, I think that says it all. I can't even begin to tell you how many goals I have set, only to have them fall by the wayside. The individual goals were always very well intended, yet they never seemed to come to fruition. Over time I started to figure out why some goals were achieved, while others were not. There appeared to be a pattern to the goals that were transformed into success or achievement. Each and every one had a plan. I began to realize that a goal with a plan was a goal that was achieved. A goal *without* a plan was lost and generally forgotten.

Some of my goals, the biggest ones, were accompanied by a plan that allowed me to achieve it. Making a million dollars a year, even in difficult business times was possible because when I set that goal, I didn't stop there. I immediately followed it up with a plan. I created a list of step-by-step actions that I would follow until I achieved the result I desired.

When I was 31 years old, I ran a marathon. Twenty-six point two straight miles can sound daunting if you get too far ahead of yourself. I didn't wake up one day, throw on a pair of running shoes and step out onto the road. I didn't make a million dollars in one year by waving a magic wand. I didn't lose 30 pounds and keep it off for over ten years to date simply by snapping my fingers. I didn't get my high school diploma, go to college for 12 years, create a radio program, develop speaking programs, write a book, or start a charity by accident. Everything I have accomplished can be attributed to one thing. Making a plan. Well, two things. The desire to succeed and developing a plan to make it happen.

Succeeding at anything is simple. But that doesn't necessarily mean it is always easy. My successes were by no means easy – I don't think anyone's are. With proper planning and determination, anything is possible. Even the most difficult goals can be achieved if they are approached the right way.

As I was saying earlier, when I was 31 I ran a marathon for the first time in my life. I trained for several months and then something happened I hadn't planned for. I came down with the flu two days before the race. So my plan and my training needed to be quickly modified. I rested and drank a lot of fluids. "How am I going to run 26.2 miles with the flu?" I asked myself over and over again. The answer came to me one day when I was reviewing my plan. I would run the marathon one step at a time – just like my plan was written.

Flu or no flu I knew I wanted to go out and try. I was determined to do my best which that day may or may not have gotten me over the finish line, but God as my witness I was going to give it everything I had. And I did. Now let me tell you, by the sixth mile I was already hurting. My body was sore and stiff. I had to keep stopping and stretching. I had absolutely no idea how I was going to make it another 20 miles. Finally, I made the decision. My new plan was to not stop until I literally could not go another step. For the next 20 miles I kept repeating to myself "I can go one more step. I can go one more step." Four hours later, one step at a time, I crossed the finish line.

When I set the goal for running a marathon I also made a plan to make it happen. The plan was pretty simple and went like this:

Step One: Join a training group
Step Two: Choose the marathon I wanted to run

Step Three: Get the right gear – shoes, clothing, orthotics, etc.
Step Four: Train
Step Five: Run

Once I put it into those little bite size daily steps, it was pretty simple to do. Were you going to get back to your happy, healthy, and feel good weight? Were you going to get your degree, make more money or get a better job? Any and all of these are possible, which I'm sure you already know. So, if they are possible, why have you not done them? My guess is you got overwhelmed by not knowing where or how to begin. You wondered, how am I going to achieve this goal? Many times, once people realize just how much there is to do they get overwhelmed and allow that to stop them in their tracks. Boy do I know what that's like. In fact, I have enough examples to fill up the rest of this book. So, when I say I know what you're going through, that I have firsthand experience in dealing with immobilizing overwhelm I truly mean it. I'll share with you a few examples of how I faced the overwhelm head on and managed to overcome it.

Tip #21- Make a plan

Exercise 4.1

1. Write down a goal that you want to work on
2. Write down everything you need to do to accomplish this goal.
3. Write down the days/ weeks/months you have until you want to reach this goal.
4. Break down what needs to be done into monthly/weekly/daily steps.
5. Every day create a things to do list and make sure your daily item is on it.

Two things impress people most when I tell them my story. The first is how I went from making about twenty thousand dollars a year as a manicurist to making over a million dollars a year in sales a few years later. Second is that I moved from California, my home state of 35 years, to New York completely on my own.

Let's start with the move. I had lived in California my entire life but in 2005 I took a vacation to New York and absolutely fell in love with it. From the moment I stepped foot off the airplane I felt as though my soul belonged there. The feeling was unexplainable, I wasn't even in the city yet – in fact I hadn't even left the airport – yet I just felt at home. Of all the cities I'd lived in throughout California, none felt as comfortable as New York. I simply loved it. I went first to the Hamptons and then on to New York City. It amazed me that the two could be so close but so different.

There was not a single thing I didn't like about Manhattan. I loved the hustle and bustle. I loved that there were so many people in a fairly small space and everyone co-existed peacefully. It didn't matter if you were a stock broker, an actor, a business person, or a bum on the streets. Everyone existed together and simply went about their business with no judgment, no intolerance. I loved that I didn't have to drive anywhere – a refreshing change from the gridlock in California.

After just one day in New York City, I was in love. I went back to visit three more times in 2006. On Christmas Day, I was visiting with my only two friends in New York and I said, "I have an announcement to make. I'm moving to New York and my goal is to be here by the end of February 2007." Of course they thought I was absolutely insane. I am sure they wondered if I was really going to do it and probably thought I was just caught up in the holiday spirit of New York City.

Little did they know, I was serious. I had moved before on my own but never across the country. Where does one even begin such a task? This is where the plan started to take form. On the flight back to California I did what I knew worked best and I started my moving to New York City plan. It went something like this:

1. Find a place to live
2. Sell house in California

3. Sell car in California
4. Sell all possessions in California
5. Pack items to take to New York

That was about the gist of my first list. I called a new friend in New York and asked if he knew of anyone who could help me find an apartment to rent. I ended up with three names and I called them all almost immediately. Finally, after speaking to all three, I decided on the one that felt like the right fit. We coordinated schedules and figured out a time when I could fly out again to do a power search for my first New York City apartment. Mid-February I went back to New York and my new agent and I went to 15 apartments over the course of two days. The last one on the last day was the apartment for me. I signed the lease and my move in date was April 1. Step one was checked off my list.

Now for step two. I had to sell my house in California. I had maintained a relationship with the agent I used when I bought the house so I called her up and told her I wanted to sell. We met a few days later and listed my house. Less than a month later we got a good offer, and were set to close in 30 days. Things progressed smoothly with the sale and about two weeks before the closing date I knew I had to get rid of all the stuff in my house. I had three bedrooms, two bathrooms, a living room, a dining room and a kitchen to clear out in the next few weeks. It was time for a garage sale. I posted an ad in the local newspaper for the following weekend and I didn't even bother to put prices on anything. Everyone who passed through I told "Absolutely everything must go. Make me an offer." And over the next several hours almost everything went. TV, dressers, beds, dishes, office furniture and the like, almost everything was gone. I just had two big things left. A large china cabinet and a Victorian style sofa.

Now what? How was I going to get rid of these things? I thought for a moment and the idea of a consignment shop came into my head. I did a search online and found one that would pick up the items and give me a percentage of the profit when they sold it in their store. A few days later they too were gone and I only had a few details left. There were some odds and ends that I needed to get rid of so I packed them up and found the closest Goodwill. I then started to pack up the items that I was not going to need before my rapidly approaching move. I put everything in boxes and shipped them to my new address in New York.

At this point I had about a week left and I still had clothes and shoes to pack and a car to sell. Except I knew I would still need my car until almost the last minute. How can you possibly sell a car in a day or two? After a little research I found a company called Carmax that does an evaluation of what they think the car is worth and if you're happy with the offer they write you a check on the spot. And that's exactly how it worked for me. After they handed me the check I called a friend to pick me up and drive me home. At this point I was two days from my move date and just a few details away from my goal.

All I had left to do was pack the clothes and shoes I was taking with me. I like to say that I am the real life Carrie Bradshaw from Sex and the City so this part of my plan was pure comedy. Other than Sarah Jessica Parker and I sharing a birthday, I was a writer, I was going to be living in New York City and let me tell you do I love shoes! In fact, I had a closet dedicated just to shoes. There was no way on God's green earth that I was going to ship out clothes and shoes without my direct supervision. I packed five suitcases full to the brim and they were going on that plane with me. I crammed all I could into my carry-ons and everything else I checked at the airport.

That was it. April 2, 2007 I took a taxi to the airport, checked my bags and said goodbye to California. There were a lot of details involved in this move. Moving your entire life across the country is no easy task. However, it was made very simple, and almost stress free because I had a plan. Every time I thought of something I needed to do I would write it down and put it into the plan. Anytime you move you need to do little things like turn on and off the utilities, cancel insurances and other no longer needed policies, etc. Whenever I thought of something of that nature, I would write it on my list. That right there was my one and only saving grace for a stress free cross country move.

I have found that stress is usually created by the overwhelm of too many things rolling around in your head. Simply writing them down eliminates the possibility of forgetting something important – because it is already on paper. There were times that I would start to feel stressed out and each time I noticed it was because I was accumulating things in my head that I knew I needed to do. The very moment I recognized that feeling of stress or overwhelm, I got out my "to do notebook" and wrote down the new tasks. Then I'd look over that list and decide what was most practical to do first, then second, then third and so on. Task by task everything got done. Remember, I did this move by myself. I was single and living alone, and had no family living anywhere near me. I did have friends that helped me with my garage sale and gave me rides when I needed it, but for the most part everything that needed to be done was on me. A lot of people tell me this was quite the undertaking. However, truth be known, to me it really was not that big of a deal. I knew I could do anything if I made a plan and did what needed to be done by taking it one step at a time.

I believe this is possible with just about anything. Losing weight, making money, finding the man or woman of your dreams, or making a plan work. First you have to know what you want, and then you have to make a plan to help you get what you want. It really is that simple.

Let's take a moment to look at a money making example. Again, it's important for you to know that I don't just talk or write about this stuff, I live it. One year I was in sales and I said "I want to make a million dollars this year." The next words out of my mouth were "Holy Crap! How am I going to do that?" At this point in my life I knew that with a plan I could do just about anything. So, planning I did.

When it comes to making money it's almost always a numbers game. I was in sales and in order for me to make a million I had to close more deals. One day I sat down and looked at the number of deals it would take to make the million. I discovered that based on my compensation plan I needed to close 100 deals or $20 million in business per month. My average deal was $200,000. Anyone who has ever sold anything knows you don't close every deal that comes in the door. In fact, in my business it was average to close just about half of what came in the door. Therefore, in order for me to close 100 deals I needed to bring in 200. In order to bring in 200 I needed to see 400. At the time I was in the mortgage business and I quickly wondered how I would see 400 loans in one month. I looked at the calendar and determined there were, on average, 20 business days in a month. That meant I needed to bring in 10 deals per day. The problem with this was that not every customer had a deal every time I saw them so I needed to see more than 10 clients per day. I decided that I would see 15 clients per day.

Now I had my plan. All I had to do was see 15 clients per day every day. The average client visit was 30 minutes so there was more than enough time in the day to make that happen. From there, I looked at my client list and determined the most effective way to see as many clients as possible. I mapped out a route that would allow me to reach as many clients within a certain radius as possible. Each day I would go to the offices in a different area and hit as many as I could.

This plan worked like a charm! I did it. I met my goal of making a million dollars in personal income that year. The best part is it wasn't that hard to do. I knew all I had to do was see 15 clients a day and the rest would happen…and it did. When my numbers started to skyrocket, everyone wanted to know what I was doing. As others started to apply my plan, it worked for them too.

One of the best examples I can share was not my own but that of a coaching client. I met a woman who was a hair stylist. We'll call her Linda. Linda was making about $1,500 per week. This was fine for awhile but she wanted more and knew she was capable of more. We looked over her appointments from the previous few months. We added up how much she made per client for each week. We discovered she was making approximately $85 per client and averaged 19 clients a week. In order for her to reach her goal of $2000 a week she only needed to find 5 more clients a week. That's one a day. That doesn't sound so hard, right? But prior to this conversation all she knew was she wanted to make $500 more a week with absolutely no idea how to do it.

Now we know what she wanted and what it would take to get her there. The next step was to come up with the plan to get those five additional clients a week. At this point we talked about who her ideal client was. Let's say for example that Linda's ideal client was women with a single process color, cut and style every six to eight weeks. Now that we know who the ideal client is, where do those clients go now? What do they do for fun or work? Well they likely go to the gym, and get manicures and facials. Also, people come in and visit from out of town all the time and often need their hair done for a special occasion but have no idea where to go if they are not from that city.

So, we made a plan for her to get a website. Second, she had clients that she hadn't seen in awhile. A very effective way to build your business is to stay in contact with your previous clients. I recommended she call or send a letter or card to the clients that were past their hair-do date to touch base and say hello or let them know of a discount or special she was running for the month. That alone brought her in some extra clients for the week. Then we talked about getting some marketing materials such as flyers, brochures and new business cards with the website address on it. The plan was to leave it where these ideal new clients go. She started to take them to gyms where she knew trainers and was offering free or discounted services for auctions and gift bags at events. Then she approached hotel concierges about referring their guests to her. Then she committed to going to a minimum of two networking events a month so she could meet people outside her usual circles.

Almost immediately Linda started to see results. Her business was growing and she was getting exactly what she wanted. More business and more money. For months, if not years, before creating this plan,

Linda thought about growing her business, but never did anything to make it happen. That was because she never knew where to start. After just a few weeks of working with me on this new plan, she started to see results and accomplish her goal. Before she knew it she had the clients she was looking for and then some!

You see, this can work for anything. If you want to grow your business, or get in shape, or lose weight or make more money, you can if you make a plan. Figure out what you want and then what it will take to get it. Take a deep breath and do everything you can to not get overwhelmed. Remember, you aren't going to do all of it all at once. You will create the plan and then start to apply it one simple step at a time.

Now, let's add a little fun to your plan. A visual map. A visual map is like a collage with a bunch of pictures of you and your goals. When I set out to make a million dollars, I took a copy of a check and wrote my name on it and wrote in $1,000,000. I also took my previous year's W2 and put $1,000,000 on it with the current year covering the previous year. When I set the goal to run a marathon I cut out a picture from a magazine of someone crossing the finish line, only I put a picture of my face over the model's. When I decided I wanted to get my degree I took a copy of a friend's bachelor's degree and put my name on it. For every goal I set I find a picture and make it mine. I put my name or my face on it. For fitness or body goals I would cut out pictures of the body I wanted and put my head on the model's body. Now every New Year's Eve I have a Dream Board Party and have my friends come over and we put together our visual maps of all that we want for the coming year. That is a great way to start the year off right.

A couple of things to remember while you're making a plan to make your goals happen. Number one, sometimes you'll be on one path and it leads you down a completely different and totally unexpected path. When I left my job at the phone company I got another job as a secretary. I thought I wanted to be an Executive Assistant for the rest of my life. Little did I know that I was going to be exposed to sales and ultimately decide that that was a better fit for me. The point is, be flexible you never know where your plan may lead you.

The last little tip on taking your talk for a walk is to cut yourself a break. As I mentioned before, I lost 30 pounds several years ago. I had a plan on how I was going to do it. However, sometimes life got in the way and my plan went to hell. That didn't happen a lot, but it did happen. Forgive yourself for mistakes or for veering off the plan. Just cut yourself a break and get back on track. Remember to reward yourself along the way to your goals. Whether you are working towards a degree, a health or fitness goal, a job or income goal, or anything of the sort, reward yourself along the way. Have milestones and landmarks with a little something special you do for yourself when you hit a mark along the path to the end result. You will feel good and stay on the path much better and much stronger when you hit some rough patches, if you have a little something to look forward to along the way.

LESSONS LEARNED

1. Always make a plan
2. Break your plan down into daily manageable bits
3. Create a visual MAP to your goal
4. Don't worry if your MAP takes you down an unexpected path
5. Forgive yourself for being human
6. Reward yourself often

Chapter 5:
Kick Your Fear In The Rear

Fear. Now there is a four letter word. And this one has teeth. Fear can stop us in our tracks. It can prevent us from accomplishing our goals, from finding love, and it can sabotage a relationship once we've found it. It can cause us to push people away or behave in ways we never thought possible.

Many times, the things we fear only exist in our imaginations. Look up fear in the dictionary and you'll find this definition: a distressing emotion aroused by impending danger. If that's the case then why is it that fear holds us back from things that aren't dangerous? Things that won't cause us harm, death or injury? Why would we be fearful of something that could only be good for us? Logically, it just doesn't make any sense does it?

Herein lies the problem: Fear isn't logical, it's emotional. However, if we can shed some light on fear – what it is, how it works and how to deal with it when it comes up – then we can conquer it and achieve success in every facet of our lives.

What is fear? Believe it or not, in reality there are really only two types of fear. There's fear of snakes, spiders, heights, small spaces, and peanut butter sticking on the roof of your mouth. Yes, you read that last one correctly. Arachibutyrophobia is the medical term for the fear of peanut butter sticking to the roof of your mouth. There are also those other types of fears that are far more destructive to our daily lives. These are the fears that stop us from taking a chance and going after what we want. Things like the fear of failure, success, and rejection to name just a few.

Yes, all those and many others are real, documented fears. But, as I said, there are only two types of fears and each of those mentioned fit into those two categories. The two types are real fear and fake fear.

Real fear is something that could cause you physical harm or death – like fear of snakes. If a snake bites you it will most definitely be painful and could result in illness or death. Spiders? Same thing. Yet those are not the things that generally prevent us from moving forward in our lives and working toward our goals. The fears that tend to prevent us from pursuing the life we want are things like fear of failure, fear of success or fear of rejection. The strange thing is these are things that only exist in our head or in our imagination. We may think they're real because rejection feels real, failure feels real yet with every rejection or failure there was likely a lesson learned. And that's almost always a good thing. We emerge stronger or smarter because of that experience.

Fake fears don't cause physical harm or death. You don't die because someone turned you down for a date. Most of us faced rejection early on in life. In high school almost every single person got turned down or rejected by someone they had a crush on. But we survived, right? We didn't die or end up in the hospital with broken bones. Sure our feelings may have been hurt or our ego was a little bruised, but we survived. And we likely became a better person in some way because of it.

So, what's holding you back? What goals have you set for yourself that you haven't achieved? And most importantly, why not? You may have a thousand answers for that question but I want you to really get to the root and be completely honest with yourself because you don't have to share this information with anyone else. You can write your answers on a separate piece of paper and burn it after you are finished if you'd like. However, if you don't answer these questions and discover the real answers you will be doomed to repeat the same mistakes and continue to not reach your goals or have the life you want. Ask yourself some very direct questions:

Tip #22- Identify your fears

Exercise 5.1

1. What am I afraid of?
2. Why have I not achieved this goal or why did I not even try?

You can't deal with a fear if you don't know what the fear is. When you figure out what's holding you back you can shed some light on the problem so you are able to come up with a solution. It's just like having something go wrong with your car. If you don't know what's broken you can't fix it. And if you don't know the question, you can't find the answer. Eleanor Roosevelt, who is one of my biggest idols of all time said, "You can curse the darkness or you can strike a match." That is what we're doing right now. If you have been complaining that you want something to change, you want things in your life to be different but have done or are doing nothing about it, then right now we are going to turn on the light. We are going to strike a match and take a close look at what is really going on so we can correct it and move on to accomplish the great things that are possible for us.

Let me give you an example. Several years ago, when I was in my early twenties, I was working for a store in a shopping mall. I was on my lunch break and went to the food court. I was standing in line to place my order when a man at the counter turned around and we made eye contact. I swear to you, I felt as if I had just been struck by lightning. He didn't say a word nor did I. But I can tell you something happened. We had a moment. Unfortunately it was a moment neither of us acted on.

I went back to my store thinking, "What was that? What just happened?" At that moment I had never felt anything like it before. I called a girlfriend later that night when I got home. When I told her the story she inevitably asked, "Why didn't you say something to him?" Of course, I had no good answer. I had stood there and let that moment pass me by. That was almost twenty years ago, and I remember it like it was yesterday. What if…? Those thoughts went through my head for years. What if he was the one? What if he was supposed to be my husband and father of my children? What if he was my soul mate? The bottom line is I will never know the answers to those questions because I let fear stand in my way.

I can, however, tell you this: that was the last time I ever let fear get the best of me. Not knowing what this man might have said is what stopped me. The fear that he may not want me, might reject me, or tell me to go away and pound sand stopped me from talking to a man who may have been my perfect life partner. To this day, I will never know if he was the one for me. All because I let fear get in my way.

Take a moment to think of a time when you let fear get in your way. Wasn't the fear worse than reality? Most of the time, this is the case. Often when we are feeling fear we don't take action. We let the fear get in our head and stop us from going after what we want. Surely you have had a time when you felt the fear but acted anyway. And if I had to guess, your fear of the situation was far worse than the situation itself wasn't it?

Now it's your turn. Write down a goal that you have set for yourself but have not taken action on. This could be anything – getting your degree, applying for that new job, asking that special someone out on a date, losing weight…anything. Take a moment and write down your answers.

Why didn't you take action? What was getting in your way, holding you back or stopping you? Be honest here. You don't have to tell anyone else what is really going on. This is between you and you. If you want to share your fear with someone else that's okay, but the most important thing is to figure out what is happening below the surface and keeping you stuck in the muck. The funny thing is that fear causes more issues than just fear. Not only does fear hold you back from accomplishing and succeeding at the things you want, but after the fact, when you do not take action and realize that you let fear stand in your way, you then have the feeling of regret and unknowing. If you took action and stepped up to the plate you would have gotten results. Those results could be good, bad, or indifferent. Regardless of the outcome, they are still results. I believe that trying and failing is better than not trying and wondering what would have happened if you had taken action.

Now that you are aware of the fear, how can you deal with it? Your next exercise is to answer the following questions. You will find it more effective if you actually write them down rather than simply thinking about them.

Tip #23- Come up with ways to conquer your fears

Exercise 5.2

1. What is the fear you are facing?
2. Name 5 things you can do to make the fear less intimidating.
3. Write down the 5 worst things that could happen. Are they really that bad?
4. Write down the 5 best things that could happen.
5. Break what you want down into 5 baby steps that do not feel intimidating.
6. Assign a day and tell someone to ask you at the end of the day if you completed that first step.
7. Do. Go through your list of baby steps and do them one at a time.
8. Repeat number 7 until all steps are complete, then make a new list of another 5 steps.

Now you have a plan that can help you work past the fear you feel. Do this anytime you find yourself getting paralyzed by fear so you can take action.

When I was an Executive Assistant making three grand a month I was scared to death to make the move to sales. What did I know about sales? Next to nothing was the answer. One thing I did know, however, was that I could always go back to being a secretary. I could always go out and get another three thousand dollar a month job. If I didn't make the jump to sales I would have always wondered what could have happened if I had only given it a shot.

As you already know I moved from California to New York completely on my own. At the time I made the decision to move, I knew two gay men on the island of Manhattan, that was it. I worked from home so I didn't have colleagues or associates to connect with as a means of meeting new people. Let's face it; I was pretty much on my own. I can't count the number of people who have asked how or why I would leave the comfort of my life in California for whatever it was I hoped to find in New York. All I knew was that I had an itch to live in New York. I had always been fascinated with the City. When *Sex and the City* and *Cashmere Mafia* came out I was drawn to it even more. Then, after a couple of visits I was hooked.

My philosophy went like this: I'm moving to Manhattan. I'm not legally bound to it for life. I can go, try it out and see if I like it. If I don't I can always move back to California or anywhere else for that matter.

If I didn't go, if I didn't try it out, I would have always had in the back of my mind "What if I had gone to New York? What would have happened? Who would I have met? What would I have done? How would I be different?" To me, wondering what if was worse. I would rather give it a shot and say, "I just couldn't make it in New York," than spend the rest of my life wondering what could have happened. Now, I never have to wonder.

Another example comes from one of my former coaching clients. She had an outside sales job and was deathly afraid of walking into strangers' offices to ask for business. One day we went through an exercise which determined she was afraid of two primary things: failure and rejection. Bringing it even closer to home, she was really afraid of proving her parents right when they said that she would never amount to anything. She actually said that she "can't" walk into potential client offices and ask for business. Now, you will read more about can't versus won't in Chapter 9, but for now let's just say this: there is a big difference between can't and won't. Can't means that you physically cannot do something. Won't means you are not willing to do what it takes to do it. When this client said she "can't" walk into an office and say "Hi my name is…", I asked if she really meant can't. The question, of course, confused her a little and she quite literally said "Huh?" I replied "Are you saying you are not physically capable of walking to a door sticking out your hand, turning the knob, opening the door, walking in and saying hi my name is Mary?" She then answered yes, she was capable of doing that.

I asked her what she was really afraid of. Through further conversation we discovered that her real fear was being a failure just like her parents had said and getting rejected like she felt she had been by her family her entire life. By the end of the conversation she realized that by not taking action she was ensuring her failure and ultimately creating the reality that her parents said she was destined to become. Also, I helped her realize that if someone said no to her or her product that it was their issue, not hers. We sometimes have a way of making things be about us that, in reality, truly aren't. We have no idea what is going on in other people's lives, what's on their minds or what's happening in their world. Those are the reasons someone would say no to you or your product. None of them have anything to do with you. Don't let other peoples stuff get to you and stop you from getting what you want.

In the end, so what if someone rejects you. So what! When you are rejected you don't die, you don't end up in the hospital, your legs aren't broken, nothing bad happens. Unless, you let it. Realistically there is no danger in rejection. The only thing that can get damaged is your ego and even then, only if you allow it. If you take it personally and let someone else's issues get to you then you – and only you – are allowing your ego to get bruised.

Fear of failure and rejection are fake fears. When you shift your perspective and see fake fear for what it really is, which is nothing or a game you play in your head, it takes the power away from it. Fear can only hold you back and get a grip on you if you let it. That's why I like to look at it under a big bright light. Things appear a lot scarier in the dark. By shining a light on it you can see it really isn't all that scary after all. Just think back to when you were a child and were likely at some point afraid of the dark. You can't see what's real and what's not causing your imagination to run wild. But the moment the light is turned on you see everything is fine. You see what is real and how what you thought was scary really isn't.

I once worked with an aspiring actor/comedian. He was a waiter by day and wannabe actor by night. After one coaching session he was taking action. When we met he said he was an actor but didn't have any headshots, wasn't auditioning etc. We talked about what was holding him back. We realized that he had a fear of success and a fear of rejection.

Almost everyone knows that the acting world is competitive and can be filled with rejection. So you have to be really tough to stay strong and positive and keep going out and following your passion. If you are truly passionate about being an actor you have to do hundreds, if not thousands, of auditions and constantly work to improve your craft. When this man talked about acting his face lit up and you could tell it truly was his passion. It wasn't something he was just dabbling in. With all his heart, he wanted to be an actor.

For many, the fear of success is a little confusing. After all, who would be afraid of success? That's what makes this such an interesting fear. Success brings you some things you might not have bargained for. If you're an actor and you make it big, you may lose your privacy and probably won't be able to go out to dinner without being swarmed by dozens of people. If you achieve success at anything there will be certain things that are expected of you. And that pressure can get the best of a person. If you realize that there are going to be certain expectations others will have of you, but you are still willing to step up to the plate and accept them, the fear of success usually goes away.

The opposite can also happen. Sometimes, when you realize what you can expect when you get what you want, you may not want all that comes with it. So, you really have two choices. You can look at the big picture and say "I'm okay with all that goes along with achieving my goal." Or, you can say "it's not worth it and I don't want all this if it comes with that." Then again, you could also say "I don't know if I will be okay with all the stuff but I am going to do it anyway. If I get it all and don't want it all then I can walk away." Yet no matter what choice you make you will never have to wonder what if.

After this conversation my client realized he did want to achieve his goal of being an actor and maybe he would be okay with all the things that came along with it, and maybe he wouldn't be, but he was willing to take a chance and find out. That way he didn't ever have to wonder what if.

The rejection fear was only a small part of what was holding him back from taking action. Regardless, it was still present. When we got into discussing this fear he remembered that horrible feeling he left with every time he was turned down for a part. He said the rejection eventually got to be too much and he finally stopped going to auditions. I gave him a few examples of people that were rejected over and over again before they got they hit their first home run:

Mark Victor Hansen and Jack Canfield were turned down by 140 publishers before *Chicken Soup for the Soul* was picked up by a publisher.

JK Rowling, the author of the Harry Potter series, was turned down by 12 publishers before she was given the green light by lucky number 13. And even then the publisher told her to get a day job because there was not a lot of money to be made in children's books. In less than five years, she went from living on welfare to not just becoming a multi-millionaire but also the first US dollar billionaire from a children's book.

There are stories galore of struggling actors who finally got their big break that put them on the map. For example Julie Roberts who is now one of the highest paid actresses of all time, was in bit roles for five years before her big hit with *Pretty Woman*. Same goes for Jim Carrey. He did small parts for ten years before he landed the role on *In Living Color*. Then it took another four years before he got the role in *The Mask*. Who knows how many auditions these actors went on before they finally got their big shot.

In the end, this client came to the awareness that rejection was just part of the game and it didn't mean he wasn't a good actor it just meant he hadn't found the right role yet. We mapped out a plan for him to start taking action right away. The next day he powered through it with a new found passion and determination. He scheduled head shots, got in touch with his old agent, started back up with acting classes and scheduled a few auditions for the upcoming weeks. A few months later he was doing stand up and was getting some commercial roles. Most importantly, he was happy to be following his passion once again. We don't know if he will make it big or not. What we do know is that he took action to get what he wants and in the end will never have to wonder what would have happened if…

Please know that everything is not always going to happen the way you want it to. Even so there is a lot to be said about making the effort and not letting fear stand in your way even if you don't get the results you want. I know the examples I have shared with you are ones that worked out the way I or my clients wanted them too. However, that has not always been the case. I would like to share with you some other experiences that did not work out as I had planned but I still took action and had no regrets.

Several years ago I was in an airport with a friend. I saw a man traveling with his teenage daughter who was talking on the phone. He was clearly intelligent and quite sharp. He was attractive and carried himself well, and you could just tell that he had a great relationship with his daughter. When he was alone for a moment I told my friend I was going to introduce myself to him. She instantly said "Are you crazy? You're going to approach someone you don't even know in an airport? What if he blows you off or doesn't give you the time of day?" During the conversation with my friend, the man disappeared and I lost my chance to introduce myself to him. Instantly I was upset with myself because I let my friend talk me out of something and began to doubt myself. After what she said I lost my confidence and did not take action.

A few minutes later we were boarding our plane and were heading back to Orange County, California. As we were waiting for our luggage I saw the man again. This time I looked at my friend and said, "Don't say a word, I'll be right back." I grabbed my business cards and walked straight up to man I had seen. I reached out to shake his hand and said "Hi. My name is Sharmen Lane and I saw you in the airport in San Francisco. You seem like someone I would like to get to know better. If you live somewhere near here, are single, available and interested, give me a call." He reached out, shook my hand, gave me his name and said "nice to meet you, I'll call you." We chatted for a couple minutes and then I went back to my friend. She gave me the biggest hug and said "Shar, you are so rad!"

On the drive home she asked me what went through my head to bring myself to approach this stranger. In a nutshell I said that I believe you have to take action to get what you want. I wanted to meet my soul mate and be in a lifelong relationship. There was something about this man that I was attracted to and I wanted to find out if he was the one. I would rather take action and not get the results I was looking for than always wonder what if. This man could have been destined for me. He could have been my future husband and father of my children. I wanted to know if that was the case. If not, that was ok too. I would move on and keep looking, but at least I didn't have to wonder what would have happened if I had not taken action.

Now, I'm sure you are wondering what happened with Airport Man. Several days later he did call. We scheduled a time to meet. Ultimately he had to cancel but we rescheduled. Unfortunately, I had to cancel this time. We scheduled one more time, he again had to cancel and we never rescheduled after that. For whatever reason, this just wasn't going to happen. The good news is, I tried. I stepped out of my comfort zone and went after what I wanted. To this day I have no regrets. I never wonder what would have happened if…

This next example is one that most people would dread, and why many let fear get in their way. I approached a man in a restaurant at the bar when I was out with a friend. He was also with what appeared to be a friend. I had overheard their conversation and it seemed as if they were out for an after work drink. As they paused in their conversation I stepped in and said "excuse me gentlemen, forgive me for interrupting." I turned to the one I was interested in and said "Hi, I'm Shar and I noticed you from across the room. I'd love to have the opportunity to know you better.'" He looked me up and down, looked back at his friend, not at me and said, "No thanks, I only date beautiful women." I said (with the grace of a Duchess I might add) "Very well. Good luck to you." Then, I smiled at him and went back to my friend.

She asked what happened and was shocked and appalled when I told her what he had said. I wasn't shaken in the least. She asked how I could be so calm and not the least bit upset by what he had said. I replied with these exact words. "This has nothing to do with me. He doesn't know me and any man with such brazen arrogance is not a man I want to spend my time with. He clearly is not the man for me."

Both of these are examples of things that didn't work out the way I wanted them to. I could write an entire book of stories about similar situations I or others I know have experienced. In the end, the only thing that matters is that I don't let fear stand in my way. Some times are harder than others, but I ultimately take a deep breath and say "rejection is better than regret or wondering what if." The last thing on earth I would want is to end my life thinking of all the opportunities I had missed because I allowed fear to get the best of me.

I truly hope that you now have a completely different idea of fear and how you can work past it to really make your life come to life. Real fear causes physical harm or death, fake fear stops you from getting what you want and fills you with regret and the desire for second chances to do things differently. Second chances rarely happen. Shine light on your fears, put them in their place and take action to create the life you want.

LESSONS LEARNED

1. The truth about fear and how you can overcome it
2. A new way to look at fear in order to power past it
3. The difference between fake fear and real fear
4. Identify your fear so that you can overcome it

Chapter 6:
What You Feel You Make Real

Emotions rule the world. They can start wars or create life. They can make you cry or give you side stitches from laughing out loud. Passion can move one to commit murder or give a mother super human strength to save or help her child.

There is a tool you can use to fuel your emotions and accelerate your path to success. It's called energy. Fast or slow, or anywhere in between, energy is all around us all the time. We are energy. The clothes we wear, the chairs we sit on, the feelings we have – all are energy.

Every one of us can learn how to tap into energy to make good things come into our lives. However, we can also use that energy to draw in the negative. It's interesting because we tend to think that bad things just happen, and we cause the good things to happen. Truth is we make both negative and positive things happen. We attract what we do and do not want into our lives with our energy. We make what we feel, real. And that can be good, bad or indifferent.

Have you ever been on a roll in your life when good thing after good thing keeps happening? This is because your feelings have energy and when you are feeling good you are drawing in more and more of those good things. The snowball effect can also happen in reverse.

There are other times when bad things keep coming at you and no matter what you do you simply cannot seem to make it stop.

Again, everything is energy – what you think about you bring about. I know you have had a time when you were thinking of someone and the next minute they called or contacted you in some way. You were thinking of a song you like and it suddenly comes on the radio. You are looking for solution for something and finally give up and the moment you do you see and ad on TV or in the paper or what have you with the exact thing you were just looking for.

Surely you've had those times when you did not want something to happen and the next thing you know the exact thing you didn't want to have happen…happened. For example, you are walking down a hill and thinking "I hope I don't fall. I hope I don't fall." Next thing you know, gadunk, you fall. Recently, a friend of mine and I rented a car and needed to get it back by a certain time to avoid late charges. We could have made it but boy it would have been close. My friend said, "we're not going to make it." Now, I seriously thought we really had a chance to make it. It was going to be close, but it was still possible. A few more times over the next several minutes she said again "we're not going to make it." I, however, continued to say, "it will be close but we can make it." Not but a moment later she said "dammit I just missed our exit." Regardless of whether or not we could have made it, we certainly were not going to now.

Now, I am not blaming my friend or making her wrong or bad. What I am saying is that by saying, believing, and most importantly feeling that we weren't going to make it we "coincidently" missed the exit, therefore ensuring we weren't going to make it. This makes me believe even more that what we feel we make real. She truly felt as if we were not going to make it and the events that occurred after that ensured that we wouldn't.

Conversely, I have had times where an unexpected difficult situation turned into a positive one – exactly as I had pictured it. For example, I once had a terribly bad, nasty breakup with a boyfriend and we still worked for the same company. I was based in Southern California and he was in Northern California. I had heard from a friend that he was going to be attending the Christmas party for my office instead of his. Let me tell you, my stomach turned over and then twisted into knots the moment I heard that bit of information. I had just a couple weeks to prepare myself. It was almost inevitable that we would run into each other. I kept imagining myself looking and feeling more stunning than I have ever looked or felt before. Every day I imagined myself running into him and having the grace of a duchess. For the next few weeks I went through this visualization exercise and saw myself as poised, graceful and confident. I meditated, I wrote in my journal I said it out loud and in my head. Over and over I repeated and felt how it would feel to run into him yet remain composed and confident. Every single time I would get that nervous knot in my stomach I would close my eyes, take a deep breath, visualize the situation and say "I have the grace of a duchess."

Christmas party evening rolled around. A girlfriend and I went together as we were both recently single girls and her ex was also likely to make an appearance as well. We were each other's support system. By this time I was feeling rather calm and very duchess like. At any moment when if I felt slightly anxious, I would again take a deep breath and remind myself: "I have the grace of a duchess."

Inevitably the moment of truth came. I was talking to someone, turned my head and there he was. Without any thought at all, I comfortably and casually smiled, then turned away. A few minutes later my girlfriend and I went into the restroom and as we were walking out he was standing right there in front of me. Again, without any anxious or nervous feelings, I just stood still with my head held high and proud – and smiled. He stood there in front of me for what felt like an eternity, stuttering, making feeble attempts at formulating a sentence and when no words ca   e turned and went into the men's room. Speechless. I truly felt as if I had the grace of a duchess and I could not have asked for a more perfect moment. At that very moment I knew more than ever I could create and attract exactly what I wanted.

We all have ensuing situations that we know could be uncomfortable for a multitude of reasons. The technique I described above is good for all sorts of those moments. Remember – what you feel you make real. Once upon a time I was dreadfully afraid of flying. I would white knuckle even the shortest flight. Then I discovered the Law of Attraction and applied it to this very situation. Before a flight I would visualize the plane taking off, flying smoothly through the air and smoothly landing on the runway. Sometimes I would imagine God's hand holding the plane and placing it gently on the runway. While I imagined this I would repeat in my mind, over and over again "smooth comfortable flight, soft easy landing." To this day I am amazed at how relaxed and comfortable I instantly become, just by repeating that phrase. Now when I fly, I have no anxiety at all. If there is turbulence I can honestly say I don't notice it unless it is abnormally bumpy. If I feel the slightest sense of nervousness I simply take a deep breath and repeat the phrase "smooth comfortable flight, soft easy landing" again and I instantly calm down. I don't know if the turbulence stops or if I no longer notice it. Either way I get the result I'm looking for – a calm and relaxing feeling during any flight.

At one time I was interested in becoming a Phlebotomist, a medical professional that draws blood. However, this was when there was no internet so I had no idea how to find out about it. I was a manicurist at the time and had a client that worked at a local hospital. I asked her if she knew of anyone I could talk to that would give me advice on how to get started. Next thing I knew, I had a name and number of a man she thought might be able to help. I called him and he told me that most people who got into phlebotomy were working at the hospital already, doing something else, and were promoted or transferred into that department. To the best of his knowledge there were no outside training programs for phlebotomy. I searched everything and called everyone I could think of. Finally, after weeks of searching I gave up. I remember very clearly saying out loud one day, "Okay, universe. I am leaving this one to you. I have done everything I can think of and I am getting nowhere. If this is what I was meant to do then show me the way."

I continued to move on with my days. The difference was, I wasn't stressed or pushing the square peg into the round hole trying to force this thing to happen. Somehow, I simply knew the answer was going to come to me. It was just going to happen. So, I didn't do anything from that point on. Then about a week later I was standing in line in a department store and overheard a woman in front of me talking about how she just got her phlebotomy certification. My ears instantly perked up and I tapped her on the shoulder and said "excuse me, but I couldn't help but overhear you just say you just got your phlebotomy certification. I have been searching high and low to find a training program and have not been able to. Would you mind sharing with me the name of this program?" She answered "It's called the Phlebotomy Group and it's in Sherman Oaks." I thanked her and we both went our separate ways. The moment I got home I called information and asked for the number. Low and behold, I now had the number for which I had been looking for, for weeks.

Within days of my feeling that it was going to somehow happen and releasing it to the universe, the answer came to me. This is exactly how many of the most amazing things happen to us. And that is exactly how this chapter came about. What we feel we draw more of into our lives. That is why when you are in a bad mood bad things seem to happen. Have you ever been having a sad moment that turns into a sad hour and then you next thing you know the whole day is gone and you feel down and depressed and worse than ever? If you aren't careful you can sit on the sofa and do nothing and fall deeper and deeper into depression. That is something that has likely happened to all of us. However there is a way, there are several ways, to get out of the funk and feel good and create the things you want in your life. You need to feel the feelings you want to have so you can make the things you want real.

The big question is how? How do you get the feeling you want without having the thing you actually want? This is why it is so important to get control of your feelings because what you feel you make real. You want to start feeling what you want, not what you don't.

There are several techniques you can use. Meditation, visualizations, journaling, sharing, EFT, trigger devices, anchoring techniques, and the list goes on.

I have learned to feel what I want to make real. So often we get caught up in our unrealistic emotions. We let our fears get the best of us and have our minds running out of control. This exercise can calm you down and help you to get what you want.

Tip #24- Visualize the end result

Exercise 6.1

Step 1: Close your eyes and roll your eyeballs under your lids as if you were looking upward.

Step 2: Slowly count from 100 down to one, seeing and saying each number in your mind.

Step 3: With your eyes still rolled back as if you are looking upward, see a picture or an image of what you want.

Step 4: Feel it! While holding that image in your mind, feel how it would feel if you had it. Feel the excitement the energy the happiness, joy, elation, relief, calm or whatever emotion you want to have.

Step 5: Stay in the feeling while seeing the image as long as you can. The longer you can feel that feeling and see that image together the faster it will manifest in your life.

This may be difficult for some because there are those that just can't imagine how to feel an emotion about something they don't have yet. To help you with this you can do the following exercise. However, before I share this with you I want tell you about a time this worked for a client who was nothing short of amazed at the results.

We all have to deal with uncomfortable situations at some point in our lives. However, we can make it much easier if we simply use the power of our feelings, changing the energy to get the result we want. I was working with a client who had just married a man that was divorced and had a young daughter. His ex-wife was, according to my client, very difficult. The ex-wife was remarried yet still wanted nothing to do with the new wife. My client, the new wife, was not allowed to go to ballet recitals, school plays, birthday parties etc. The husband was trying to keep the peace with both the new wife and the ex- wife which was, obviously, a difficult task at best.

The yearly vacation was on the horizon. The ex-wife was going to be there with the daughter for the first week and then the husband and new wife were going to take the next week. The ex-wife had requested that the new wife not be in the room when they switched. This didn't go over very well with my client. The husband told the ex-wife this was unreasonable and that his wife would be present. After much back and forth it was decided this is how it was going to be. I told my client to imagine the vacation transition with the ex-wife exactly as she wanted it to be. Then I had her think of a time when she really felt calm, relaxed, serene – as if she didn't have a care in the world. She said she was thinking of when she gets a massage and is listening to the ocean sounds playing softly in the room as she's starting to drift off to sleep. When she had the image in her mind I told her to feel the same feeling of relaxation and comfort like when she gets a massage. Then we created an affirmation to go along with it. It went something like this: "Smooth calm transition where everyone is comfortable and relaxed."

For the next month she visualized this image in her mind while feeling a sense of calm and serenity repeating the phase, "Smooth calm transition where everyone if comfortable and relaxed." Anytime she felt uneasy about the upcoming situation she would simply take a deep breath and repeat that affirmation. The closer the day came, the more relaxed she felt.

Transition day arrived and she felt more relaxed about it than ever. She had a sense of knowing that it was all going to be alright. Together, she and her husband walked through the door and his daughter rushed to them both and gave them a big, warm, and happy hug. The ex-wife said hello and everyone opened up to conversation. The ex-wife was talking to the new wife as if she were her new best friend. She was sharing stories of the week and telling her where the new hot spots were. She even wrote out a couple of notes and showed her references in a travel guide book. After about 30 minutes had passed, the ex-wife said it was time for her to be going. She said goodbye to her daughter, told the couple to have a great time, smiled, waved and headed out the door.

The moment the door closed behind her the couple looked at each other and said, "was that the same person we know?" They were both shocked and amazed at how comfortable and relaxed everyone was. They could not have asked for a more perfect transition and wondered if the ex-wife was on medication because she had never been this nice or pleasant.

My client came back from her vacation and felt more empowered than ever before. She started to use this technique at work, with her own family, with any situation she thought might be remotely uncomfortable. Every now and again she would not get the results she was looking for but she admitted it was because even though she had the image in her mind she did not really hone into the feeling she wanted. When she remembered that, she would apply it the next time and reported that when she truly felt the feeling she always got the results she was looking for.

Now it's your turn. Read below, follow these steps and apply them to an upcoming situation that you are facing.

Tip #25- Feel "as if" you had what you want

Exercise 6.2

Step 1:   Think of a time that you were on top of the world. A time when you felt unstoppable and as if nothing could get you down. Or, think of an upcoming situation and the emotion you are seeking. Write that moment down on a piece of paper. Sometimes this is hard for people to do so the best thing to do is imagine the situation occurring exactly the way you want it to and feeling how you want to feel when it happens.

Step 2: State what your current reality is. What is going on in your life that you want to be different? Whatever it is, just write it down.

Step 3: Now write down what you want. No judgment, no opinion. Just write want you want.

Step 4: Imagine you had what you wrote down for Step 3 and feel the feeling you had in Step 1.

Step 5: Stay in that feeling and stay there for as long as you can.

Step 6: Repeat this every day. The moment you wake up and right before you go to bed. Or any other time when you feel you need it.

There are still a few more tools you can use to help you get in the right mindset to achieve your goals. You may want to use all of these or just select those that are right for you. Personally, I find the one that works best for me and I pretty much stick with it. However, if I am facing something really important I will use them all to really lock it in.

This next exercise should get you familiar with anchoring techniques. It's a tool you can use in just one simple step to instantly change your mood. It works like the flash button on your phone or the last button on your television remote. You can even think of it as a remote control for your mind.

Anchoring is the process by which a particular state or response is associated with a unique anchor. An anchor is most often a gesture, voice tone or touch. It has been said that by recalling past resourceful states one can anchor those states to make them available in new situations.

Follow the steps below and create an anchor for yourself.

Tip #26- Use an anchor to shift your state of being

<u>Exercise 6.3</u>

Step 1: Remember a time when you felt great, on top of the world, as if you could do no wrong. Close your eyes and imagine that moment again. What were you wearing, how did you look and feel? Go back to that time as vividly as you possibly can as if you can see, touch and feel it all over again.

Step 2: Do something physical like touch your pinky and thumb together or squeeze your earlobe, snap your fingers, etc.

Step 3: Every time you feel another moment like that, perform your physical connector again to really lock it in. For example, if you choose to pinch your earlobe do it again and again every time you feel that same strong emotion.

Step 4: When you are in need of a pick me up or need to quickly adjust your attitude or frame of mind, use your anchor. Pinch your earlobe or touch your pinky and thumb together. This will instantly trigger your mind and emotions to feel that happy, good feeling that you have already anchored.

You may not always have the time or space to close your eyes and count back from 100 or write down your situation and create an affirmation, but the anchoring technique can be done anytime, anywhere. The trick with this technique is to really lock in that positive emotion and connect it with a physical touch over and over again. Every time you have an incredible and extraordinary feeling that you want to be able to remember and use in any situation, lock it in and anchor it while the feeling is fresh. Then you will be able to flash back to that feeling whenever you need it.

There is one last tool you can use to help you bring about what you think about. This one is called synergy. Synergy is the interaction of two or more agents or forces so that their combined effect is greater than the sum of their individual effects. In simplest terms, the sum of the whole is greater than its parts. As an example of synergy, Clydesdale horses were individually tethered to a number of barrels and tested to see how much weight they could pull. The results were recorded. Then, a team of Clydesdale's were tethered together and the same process was repeated and those results were recorded. Now comes the synergistic part. The weight the team pulled together was 25 percent more than the total weight the individual horses pulled earlier.

What does this mean and how can you make it work for you? I would like to show you how to combine the strengths of your subconscious mind with the strengths of your conscious mind to get greater or faster results.

You're conscious mind is a powerful thing. It's aware of the thing or things on which you focus your attention. The subconscious mind is extraordinarily powerful and remembers everything you have ever seen, heard, tasted, touched, and felt. Under proper hypnosis everything you have ever seen, heard, felt, etc can be remembered. The subconscious mind is aware of everything that goes on behind the scenes. Things of which you may not be fully cognizant. Most of us know that things can be buried so deep in our subconscious mind that we have no idea they ever existed in the first place. Everything we have seen, touched, tasted, felt is all stored in this hard drive in our mind. Your subconscious mind records everything whether you are aware of it or not. Hypnosis has been used to solve crimes to help one remember things they didn't realize they saw or heard in the first place.

On the other side of your subconscious mind is your conscious mind. Some call this your awareness, or your consciousness. It is aware of everything you are giving your full attention to. There are many people that believe they are great multi-taskers. However, studies have shown that when one is multi-tasking their IQ actually drops. Even though we think we can do several things all at once truth is we really are not as efficient as we think. One thing we can do to improve our effectiveness in creating the things we want is to combine the strength of our conscious and subconscious mind so they can work together to help us achieve anything.

Your subconscious mind does not know the difference between what is real and what is fake. For example, think about your dreams – or better yet, your nightmares. I remember once, years ago, I was dreaming that I was being chased by a man and I was running trying to get away. I climbed a ladder that put me on a rooftop. The man followed. He ultimately caught up with me and cornered me on the ledge where I had nowhere else to go. He put his hands around my throat and started to squeeze. I could barely breathe and was struggling trying to break away. I lost my footing and slipped off the ledge. I started to fall and just before I hit the ground I woke up screaming and my body jerked as if I had just hit the ground. Then, I awoke.

I remember I was sweating, breathing heavy, my heart was pounding. My body was responding to something that wasn't real. My subconscious mind thought it was real but when I woke up I realized it wasn't real at all. Now the question is, how does this help you?

By using repetition and emotion you can tap into the power of both your conscious and subconscious mind. This then creates synergy and allows for a combined effect that is greater than using one or the other independently. Again, the question is how? How do you create synergy between your conscious and subconscious mind?

As we have already discussed, the conscious mind is aware of things we give our attention to. The subconscious mind is aware of everything. A trigger device can help you make this connection. You can use a color coding dot – one of those stickers that are found in most office supply stores, or simply use the end of a felt tip pen or marker. First you need to associate your trigger with a meaning. I recommend putting your sticker or dot on a blank piece of paper. Once you have your trigger you need to write a statement of what you want but you must write it in the positive and present tense. I have found it works best if you start with I am… or I'm grateful… and then proceed to write what you want as if you already had it.

For example, I have written "I'm grateful that I am a world famous author and speaker." After writing that statement next to the dot on the blank page I concentrated on it and felt what it would feel like if I had it and then I took those colored dots and placed them all over my home.

I put those little dots everywhere. On the coffee pot, microwave, bathroom mirror, television, lamp, remote control, etc. Everywhere my eyes looked. Over time I really didn't even see them anymore. However, even though I wasn't giving these dots my attention, my subconscious knew what they meant. When I wrote that, I had never spoken outside the U.S. Within days of writing and placing my color coding dots all over my home I received a phone call to speak in Malaga, Spain. I also received several orders for my book in India, Japan, and Germany. Shortly thereafter I was doing an event in St. Kitts in the Caribbean.

Another affirmation or "I Am" statement I've used is when I was working to lose a few extra pounds. This time I used this statement, "I'm at my ideal body weight and maintain it with ease." Almost immediately people started to comment that I had lost weight. I'm not one that is really concerned with the scale but I have to say my clothes started fitting looser and I liked the way I looked in the mirror. I personally prefer starting my affirmations with "I'm grateful..." because I instantly feel a sense of calm and knowingness of what I'm wanting to attract into my life. I feel as if I have it already the moment I say I'm grateful for it.

This is your last exercise for this chapter. Try this one and see how it feels for you.

Tip #27- Use a trigger device

Exercise 6.4

Step 1:   Choose your trigger. Get a sticker, like a color coding dot or something similar and get 20 or more of the exact same thing. Or, you can simply use a felt tip pen.

Step 2: Place the mark or sticker, or whatever you have chosen, on a blank piece of paper.

Step 3: Write your "I am…" or "I'm grateful…" statement next to your trigger. Remember to keep it positive and present tense as if you already have it.

Step 4: Place your trigger all around you. On the coffee pot, on your phone, refrigerator, lamp, lightswitch, microwave, etc. Choose places you will consciously see all the time.

Doing so will connect the subconscious and the conscious minds to accelerate your goals into reality. Every single time I have used this on myself and with others there are results almost instantly.

You have been given several tools to help you believe so you can receive. Remember, the common denominator here is feelings. Feel what you want to make real. That is the main point to anything you want to attract into your life. The Law of Attraction is all about feeling what you want as if it already existed so it can manifest. Find the tool, technique, or strategy that works best for you and feels right, then take action! Nothing will work if you don't take action. Get busy and start now, so you can get to wow.

LESSONS LEARNED

1. How to use the Law of Attraction
2. The importance of visualization
3. How to flip the switch and use emotions to get what you want
4. Enhancing and expediting your results with Trigger Devices and Anchoring Techniques

Chapter 7:
Choices Change Your World

Choices are one of our most powerful tools. While this may be a tough chapter to read I implore you to read it and finish it no matter how strong your desire to resist. It is very difficult to accept that you are where you are because of your choices. No matter what, even when your choices were limited, you always had them. Sometimes you made the best choice between the options you had, but you had a choice nonetheless. Getting to a place where you are able to accept this reality can be incredibly empowering. In fact, this chapter alone can change your life because it can single handedly take you from now to wow. The most powerful and liberating thing to realize is that if you choose to believe that your choices got you where you are, and you are unhappy with that reality, you can also choose something different.

Why would one want to believe that they don't have choices? Could it be because if we were to believe that we have a choice, then we would have to take responsibility for where we are? As long as we are where we are because of something someone else said or did, then we aren't responsible. It isn't our "fault". We can't do anything about where we are if it isn't our fault we're there right? Wrong.

Accepting that we are who, where and what we are, because of our own choices is empowering. Once you choose to believe that you have the power to change it. That's a good thing. No, actually that is a great thing.

Let me share with you an example. Imagine you are walking in a parking lot and someone comes up from behind, holds a gun to your head and tells you to hand over your wallet. Do you have a choice? Yes, you do. No matter how bad or awful the alternative is you always have a choice. You can hand over your wallet or get your head blown off. I'm not saying that your choices are always going to be good versus bad, therefore making it an easy choice. Regardless, you still have a choice even when all the options are terrible. In this example the choices were bad and worse. The smart or logical choice is to hand over your wallet. That decision will have its consequences but it was the best choice to make at the moment.

I have a client who had his own catering company and was often at the disposal of his clients. He would get calls to do last minute jobs. He had big goals that he was looking to achieve and they all required an investment of money. The interesting thing was that every time he got a call which interrupted his other plans he would say "I have to take this job, I don't have a choice." After hearing this several times I asked him why he always said "I don't have a choice." His answer was "I don't. If I want to buy a house and accomplish my other goals I have to take the jobs that come to me."

I pointed out that he could choose to not take a job. He could say no – if he chose to. Right now he simply had other priorities. Those goals took precedence over other things and there was nothing wrong with that. Sometimes he would take a job and forego his morning of sleeping in, going to the gym or spending time and money out with friends. The problem was, he felt guilty for putting those other things off to take a job so he could make the money he needed to accomplish his goals. He felt that if he said he didn't have a choice it would justify him doing what he did. He could have chosen to turn down a job and been that much further from his goal.

The most valuable point here is that we all make choices. As long as we believe we don't and instead feel that we are forced to do things against our will, then we are blaming everyone else for our circumstances. When we take a look at our lives and believe that our choices got us there – good, bad or indifferent – then we can make different choices to create the circumstances that we do want.

Here's another example. I have a coaching client that I worked with for years who struggled with depression. There were many times when he would simply sit on the sofa and let the day pass by. Things were rough. His business was slow, he had no romantic life or intimate partner, he was having family issues, so in his mind life was dark and depressing. Things were not going the way he wanted them to in any way shape or form.

One day he said that it "wasn't his fault", he was going through a depressing time and he didn't really have a choice in the matter. When he was depressed, he was depressed. I asked in return, "so you are saying you have no choice in this matter at all?" He said no, he did not. I asked him what he would do if I told him that the woman of his dreams was one block away in a restaurant on the corner. She was exactly what he had been looking for and I just met her, told her all about him and showed her his picture. And she said if he was half of what I described him to be, he is the man she has spent her life looking for. "What would you do?" I asked him. He said, "Are you serious? I would run, literally run down there right now!" "Ahhhh, interesting," I said. "So you can get off the sofa when you want to? When there is a reason to get off the sofa you are capable of getting off the sofa. Quite frankly, you can 'snap out of it' when and if you have a reason to." He instantly saw where I was going with this and ultimately agreed.

Here's the thing: I have struggled with depression myself. I know what it is like to not want to get out of bed. I also know there is that one moment of truth when I have the choice to get out of bed and move on with my day and force myself to move, breathe or pull the covers over my head and pretend the world doesn't exist. Nine times out of ten I would force myself out of bed and make myself get up and get out. Sometimes I made the choice to stay in bed and feel sorry for myself. Every time I did that, I knew I was making the choice to do so. By accepting the fact that I was choosing to be depressed and stay in bed, which only made matters worse, I would almost always force myself within an hour to get up and take some action to make my life better – as opposed to making matters worse by indulging in my personal pity party.

Another coaching client I had was in sales. Sometimes when things got rough and tough she would stay at home and mope and eat ice cream in bed without ever turning on a light. Yet somehow she always managed to make our coaching calls. One day I asked, "why are you choosing to be depressed and stay in this dark place?" She said to me, "You think I choose this? I don't choose this, it just happens sometimes and I can't do anything about it." In the meantime I was emailing a friend of mine and asked her to send my client an email saying she needed her services and could she be in her office within the hour? My client got the email while we were on the phone and she said "Shar, I have a potential sale to make, I gotta go." She was ready to dash out the door and make this sale happen. As much as I hated to crush her hopes, I said whoa whoa, slow down a minute. I then asked her for the name of the person who sent the email – to verify that it was from my friend. She confirmed it was and I said "Look at you. You were capable of getting yourself together, miraculously pulling out of your dark depression, when you wanted to or when you felt you needed to. So, do you believe now that you have a choice as to whether or not you are going to stay in bed and have a pity party or get out of bed and make the life you want happen?"

She reluctantly agreed based on the example and demonstration that she did have a choice. The great news is that she hasn't chosen to stay in bed a single day since. When she feels like crap and wants to pull the covers over her head, she forces herself to get up and do something that makes her feel good to break that cycle before it begins.

For months before that she would stay depressed go deeper and deeper in the hole until someone forced her to go to the doctor and get on medication. Now, by the power of her own choices, she doesn't pull the covers over her head anymore.

Choices are around us all the time. Sometimes they're simple and easy, other times they are akin to choosing between a rock and a hard place. A simple example is one that most people have experienced or will at some point – losing weight. Whether you gain a few extra pounds because of college finals, the holidays, or whatever, most people will struggle, or have struggled, with weight issues at some point in their lives. When looking at the choices you have, you put yourself in a position to succeed at virtually anything. If you are dieting and are looking to lose a few extra pounds, the power of choice can really help you.

Over ten years ago I lost 30 pounds and have kept 20 of it off. I decided I was a little too thin so I gained 10 pounds back simply because I wanted to. In the initial stages of letting these unwanted pounds go I used my choice philosophy to determine what I was going to eat. I love sugar. If there was a jelly bean, cookie, cake or hunk of chocolate within my reach I was all over it. When I was looking to drop a few pounds I would look at the cookie and calories and ask myself if eating the 300 calorie cookie was worth the five seconds of pleasure it gave me. I would say to myself "Sharmen, do you want the momentary pleasure of eating this cookie or do you want to stay on track and be closer to your goal?" Any time I asked myself if I was going to choose my goal versus the item I wanted to eat I would always chose my goal. I realized that I had a choice to eat what I wanted at that moment or I could choose to stay on track. There were also times when I would think, if I eat this cookie I will have to go to the gym and run on the treadmill for 30 minutes to burn it off and undo it. Is eating the cookie worth it? Never once did I choose to eat the junk when I looked at it from the perspective of making a choice.

I truly believe that our choices are empowering. When we become aware that we have a choice in nearly everything it gives us amazing influence over our own life. We are no longer at the disposal of everything and everyone around us. Choosing to believe that you have a choice can be one of the most powerful and liberating things you will ever do.

It's time to put you in the driver's seat. Follow the next exercise to help empower you to make choices that change your life.

Tip #28- Accept the belief that you always have a choice

Exercise 7.1

1. Write down something to which you have recently said "I don't have a choice".
2. Now, evaluate it and determine what the other alternatives were, no matter how unattractive they may have seemed at the time.
3. Ask yourself, what other choices could I have made instead of the one I did?
4. Now that you are aware of the choices you had, would you have made a different choice?
5. In the future, look at your choices and make the best ones possible for each situation.

The big question becomes, why would one want to maintain the mindset that they don't have a choice? What does that do for you? Well, it allows you to remain stuck is what it does. It holds you motionless and unable to do anything about the life you have and don't like. This way you can say it's not your fault, you can't help it, and this is just the way it is. But this is not true. If you choose to believe that everything just happens to you and you have no say or effect on your own life then yes, you will be stuck. You will remain unhappy. However, if you change your perspective and choose to believe that you have a choice, and all day, every day you are surrounded by choices – then, and only then, will you improve your life.

Let's say for a moment you accept the concept that you have a choice. The question then becomes how do you make better ones?

Number one, know this: All choices have consequences. Before making a definitive choice about anything, write down all the possible consequences both good and bad. Most likely you will be comfortable with all the good consequences. That part is easy. Then look at the bad ones. Are the bad really that bad and are you willing to live with all of them? If the answer is yes then you can make your choice and take action on it. If the answer is no, what choice will you make?

Let's go back to the dieting and cookie example. If you are dieting and want to reduce your size, weight, or body fat percentage you must make better choices about what you put into your mouth and body. By taking the approach of choices having consequences you will empower yourself to get the results you are looking for. When you are craving a big juicy burger, pizza, doughnut or whatever, I want you to stop and think. Think about the consequences of your choice. Is eating whatever you crave worth the consequences? Will you feel sad, angry, disgusted with yourself if you succumb to this momentary craving? Or, you can think of what you will have to do to undo the consequences of that choice. If you eat the pizza or give in to your vice, you will have to do some form of extra exercise just to get rid of the calories you consumed. Is spending that much more time on the treadmill, or working out, worth it? On the other side of that coin, you will have to live with the fact that the pants you wore yesterday are not as comfortable today, or the numbers on the scale are higher than you want them to be, or maybe the tape measure grew. If none of these results are what you want or are going to be happy with then you need to step away from the chocolate soufflé.

When you look at choices from this perspective doesn't it change how you feel about the things you used to do unconsciously? I know it does for me and most of the people I have worked with.

Here is another example. It's crazy but true. I was married. I was married to a man significantly older than me. There were things I knew I didn't like before we got married however, I told myself things would be different "after we were married." It should be no surprise that things didn't change after we got married. I loved this man more than life itself, so please do not take what you are about to read as a disparaging remark against him. I saw how he was and how he dealt with his ex-wife and I chose to believe that it would be different with me. In retrospect, I realize that I knew what I had and didn't like it. But, I was in love and wanted to believe that it would all work out. Except it didn't. I chose to ignore what was right in front of me. I have no one else but me to blame for that. It's not that he was a jerk or that he didn't do what I wanted him to. He simply did what he did; I chose to marry him knowing that I didn't really like those things.

Since that truly valuable and expensive experience, I have realized there are things we can do to make better choices. I should have asked myself before getting married, "Are you willing to live with every aspect of this man, good, bad and indifferent? If nothing about him, me or us were to change for the better and things stayed the same, would I be ok with that and be willing to live with all the things I love and all the things I don't?" For me, the answer would have been no. There were things I was not willing to live with, hence my divorce. But let me tell you, I would have been much better off personally, professionally and financially, had I not gotten married. It was a valuable lesson to learn but one that could have been avoided had I known the right questions to ask.

A friend of mine had a boyfriend who found it entertaining and enjoyable to go to strip bars with his buddies. She personally didn't care for that at all. Yet he would go and then they would argue about it later. Finally one day she finally said, "Honey, I love you and I'm not going to tell you what you can and can't do, but here's the thing – I don't think it's respectful of me or of our relationship for you to go to an establishment where you are looking and touching other naked women. I know there are some women that are okay with that and I'm sorry but I'm not one of them. I find it tasteless and disrespectful.

So, you do what you want to do, but I'm telling you that it is not something I will tolerate in my romantic relationship. You might find someone that is ok with it but I'm sorry to say I'm not, and I don't want to be."

For her, this was a deal breaker. She did not want to be with a person that went to strip clubs while they were in a relationship. What he did when he was single was not an issue, but while she was in a relationship with him she found it unacceptable. Due to our friendship, and knowing what I do for a living and my passion about choices, she asked me what I thought she should do. I said, "What you see is what you get. Are you willing to live with this person and all his habits for the rest of your life, or is it something you are willing to leave him over?" For her, she was willing to walk away.

In the end, the man believed it wasn't that big of a deal and she should just get over it. He said he didn't do it that often and he wasn't going to give it up. Knowing this, she made her choice. She decided that she did not want a partner who frequented strip clubs, especially knowing that it bothered her. It simply was not something on which she was willing to compromise. A few months later she ended the relationship and found a new partner that didn't have any deal breakers. She is now happily married.

On a completely different level, several years ago I was consulting for a mortgage company and they offered me a full time position after my three month contract had expired. The job was going to be a tough one. It was going to be ridiculously long hours with personality conflicts, and control issues. Again, not knowing the questions to ask at the time, I let my ego get in the way. I liked the title. I liked the corner office. I liked the salary. But was I willing to accept everything that went along with the job, salary, title and corner office? Honestly, no I wasn't. I darn near had to completely give up my life to do this job. I accepted the job and signed on the dotted line. A month later I resigned. What was I thinking? The good news was, I learned something that I could pass on to others to prevent them from making the same mistakes I had.

Tip #29- Eliminate the deal breakers

Exercise 7.2

1. Write down a decision you are facing now. Are you looking to get married? Are you looking at a new job? Are you thinking of having children?

2. Now ask yourself, and seriously contemplate it for a moment, are you willing to accept and do all the things that go along with what you want?

3. If the answer is yes, then great! Stay the course. If the answer is no, then figure out how you are going to end the current situation so you can have what you want and all that it entails.

So, how do we make better choices? The first step is to be aware that you have a choice in virtually everything. Accepting that concept will take you leaps and bounds toward making better choices. In addition, there are a few tools and strategies that you can implement which will help you on your journey toward making better choices and creating a happy, healthy and prosperous life.

The first is what I call the Ten Second Rule. Anytime you are faced with a decision, circumstance or situation, before you react, take a deep breath and count backwards from ten to one. This will give you ten seconds to change your instant physical or emotional reaction. Though it may not change your initial response – you may still choose to explode or say or do something you might regret. This is truly a great tool to use when you are communicating with others or are having a confrontation. So often people get caught up in the heat of the moment and choose to go down a path they may later wish they hadn't. Many times that is the result of a hasty reaction and not being aware of the things to do to help make better choices or decisions. As of now, that is no longer the case.

Think of a time when you reacted to something in a way that you later wished you could change. As great as apologies are, isn't not doing something you have to say you are sorry for, a much better answer? It happens to the best of us. Something occurs and we instantly react. We fly off the handle, yell or scream, go through the roof, jump down someone's throat or send a nasty email or text message. Then when we look at the situation again it's not quite what we thought it was. Taking a 10 second breath could have helped avoid the whole mess to begin with.

Tip #30- Think before you react

Exercise 7.3

1. Close your eyes and take a moment to remember a time when you were faced with a situation to which you instantly reacted to but later wished you had handled differently.
2. Feel what you felt at that moment. Be clear on how you reacted. What were you thinking, feeling, believing at the time? Think about your reaction and see this moment in your mind's eye.
3. Imagine that you are in the same situation again. This time instead of instantly reacting, take a deep breath and slowly count from ten down to one.

Taking another look at that same situation, what would you have done differently had you used the ten second rule? Sometimes you will have done the same thing, but most of the time taking a moment to breathe and get present completely changes your perception and your reaction. Knowing this and applying it can quickly change the choices you make and how you make them.

Many years ago when I was working in Corporate America for a mortgage company I had a situation arise with one of my accounts. It was an active account I was working with and it was transferred to another sales person in my office. One day I was working with this client and literally the next day they were assigned to someone else. I was livid. I was the highest producing and most tenured sales person in this office, region and division and I could not believe I was being treated so disrespectfully.

I called my boss, his boss, and then his boss. If attention was what I wanted, that is exactly what I got...and not in a good way. My boss was not happy with the way I handled the situation. His boss was less so and his boss even less. I lost the respect of my superiors and some of my good reputation. Oh to be able to turn back time. I made my calls to apologize, but it did not undo the damage. I had some credibility to earn back which is always a lot easier said than done. That is when I created and implemented the Ten Second Rule for myself.

I'm certain you have at least one situation similar to mine where you really wish you could go back in time and undo what you did. I had many times after that when similar situations occurred but I can assure you I handled them differently, a lot differently, from that moment forward. The Ten Second Rule is a fast and simple way to take charge of your choices and make better ones.

A coaching client once had faced a situation in a relationship that could have really used the ten second rule. This man and his wife were having an argument. Something flew out of his mouth in the heat of the moment and the second it came out he regretted it. No apology could undo what he had just said, and he knew it. He was angry and was not thinking about the consequences of his actions, or in this case, his words. When he shared this story with me, he said he needed something to stop him from seeing red and saying whatever he felt in the heat of the moment. This is when I recommended he use the Ten Second Rule in any avenue of his life where he was feeling angry.

Most people's lives are intertwined. Their behaviors are similar at work as they are at home and similar at home as they are out with friends. The Ten Second Rule can really impact and affect all areas of your life if you let it. I explained what the ten second rule was and how to use it. I said that from that moment forward anytime he found himself getting heated to pay attention and be aware. Before responding or reacting to anything to take a deep breath and consider what he is about to say. If he finds himself wanting to explode, stop instantly, breathe, count backward from ten to one and then respond.

He came back the next week for our coaching call and said he had several opportunities that week to put the Ten Second Rule into practice. He raved at how great it worked in his personal and professional life. In addition to that he said several people had commented on how relaxed he was and one even asked if he was on medication! He said all his relationships had improved noticeably that week and was anxious to continue practicing this new tool.

Note here that you can use this method in more than just your person to person communications. You can apply this to electronic communications as well. Surely you have received an email that made you want to throw your computer out the window or your BlackBerry up against the wall. I know that has happened to me more than once. For most, the first instinct is to click that reply button and blast the idiot who ticked you off. On the same note, I'm certain many, if not most, have hit the send button and instantly felt a sense of remorse. The Ten Second Rule can be very helpful here. If you are dealing with someone via text message or email I highly suggest taking that deep breath, count back from ten to one and then start to type.

Another way you can do this is to instantly type what you want but DO NOT send it. Instead, save it, close it, take a breath, count back from ten, and reopen it. Now reread the initial email. Is it really what you want to say and how you want to say it? Reread the email you typed, but read it out loud this time. Does the message express, both in verse and tone, what you want it to? If the answer is yes then send it. However, 99 percent of the time you will delete it and rewrite.

This leads us to our final tool in choices change our world. This is one of my personal favorites and I believe it to be one of the most powerful. I call it the Videotape Test. If you find yourself making poor choice after poor choice and you cannot see your way out of it, use the Videotape Test. This is a wonderful way to see yourself and your actions from an outsider's point of view. Surely you have done things in your life that you are not proud of. When you see pictures or hear stories the next day you think, "ugh what was I thinking???" Sometimes you know exactly what you are doing when you are doing it and it is not enough to stop you. Just the mere planting of this seed in your mind will instantly help you make better choices from this point forward.

How many times have you said, "Why did I do that? I know better than that!" However that wasn't enough to stop you from doing it. The Videotape Test gives you the opportunity to see the problem, correct it, and walk away before there are any consequences to pay. That truly is the beauty of this strategy. If you use it you will have far fewer regrets in your life.

Right now I want you to think of who means the world to you. Someone who, if you disappointed them, you would be devastated. This could be anyone. Mother, father, coach, teacher, boss, or mentor. I want you to imagine the look in this person's eye when you are sitting in front of them when they hear about something you did. Imagine what you would feel knowing this person is disappointed in you, has lost faith, trust and all respect for you. Who is this person?

Now comes the tough part. I want you to imagine the last time you did something that you were not very proud of. Remember what it was and how it felt the morning after, so to speak. Did you feel a sense of regret, remorse, etc? Do you wish you could turn back time and undo what you did? Now that you have that example in your head I want you to imagine the moments leading up to this event. This time, however, I want you to imagine that there is a hidden video camera recording your every move. Everything you say, every move you make is on camera.

A quick side note: don't you think if everything we did was caught on tape we would all behave differently? For instance, a few years ago I lived in a building on the 11th floor and I would take the elevator up to my apartment. There were times that I would adjust my pantyhose because I was in there alone and no one was watching. Now, mind you, I wasn't pulling my skirt up over my ears or anything but I would make little private adjustments over a few seconds while I was waiting to get to my floor or going down to the lobby. One day I was in the lobby waiting for a friend and the doorman said "are you waiting for Sally?" and I said yes. He said that she was in the elevator on her way down. I cocked my head and said "how do you know she is in the elevator?" I still remember his answer to this day: "There's a camera in the elevators. I can see her." All of the sudden I realized this man and others had seen me adjusting my undergarments more than once. I was so ridiculously embarrassed. Had I known I was being watched I would have never adjusted my pantyhose in the elevator!

Something similar happened to another client of mine. Actually, it was her husband. He was at a company event one night where everyone, including him, was drinking and carrying on. Later that year at the annual holiday party a video was shown with clips of the many events throughout the year. All the employees and their spouses were sitting at their tables watching with laughter. However, at one point my client saw a clip of her husband who was in the background of what was being taped. He was dancing with another woman, not inappropriately, well, at least not until his hand was on her derriere. My client was sitting in the audience watching and saw this. Remember, this was in the background and it wasn't really the focus of the clip, but the wife still saw it nonetheless. As you can imagine, she was not particularly happy about it either. When she mentioned it to her husband on the way home and he acknowledged that he saw it too he instantly felt guilty.

The funny thing here is that he never mentioned this little incident and didn't really think anything about it… until he saw it on tape. He said he would have never done that had he known he was "being watched." And that is the Videotape Test.

I want you to imagine that you are being taped all day, every day. All your actions are being recorded. Would you adjust your pantyhose in the elevator if you were being watched? Would you eat that cookie if you knew your trainer was going to see you? Would you flirt with that man or woman at the grocery story even though you are married? Would you run that red light or stop sign if you knew a video could prove you broke the law? Most people are not going to keep this in the forefront of their minds all the time. Most don't need to. However, you should apply this technique anytime you think even for a second that you are stepping out of integrity. If the thought "should I be doing this?" crosses your mind then you need to implement the video tape test.

To give you a start to finish example of this, my Grandmother is my be all and end all. If she were disappointed in me my heart would break. Just the thought of her not being pleased with one of my actions is enough to bring me to tears. One day I was out with some friends and someone convinced me to jump up on the bar and dance with a couple of my colleagues. I jumped up on the bar and instantly thought, "Is this something I would be proud of if I saw it on tape, much less if my grandmother saw it?" I knew I didn't want to see it, much less want my Grammie to see it. I got down off that bar just as quickly as I got up. Before I started using the videotape test I think I would have gone along with crowd and been the crazy party girl that fit in. That, however, was not who I was, nor how I wanted to be seen.

This tool can also be tremendously beneficial in your marriage or intimate relationships. I think a lot of times people behave in ways that are inappropriate, not scandalous necessarily, just a little inappropriate. And they do this many times because they don't think they will get caught. I'm sure you have heard the phrase, "Integrity is what you do when no one else is watching." I think it is human nature to take others opinions or judgments more harshly than our own. If that is the case with you then the Videotape Test is right up your alley, giving you that little edge to stay within the lines of integrity and make better choices.

If you are so much as thinking about doing something that might be perceived by some as inappropriate and you are getting sucked in by your peers, stop and think about your actions being caught on tape and then being shown to your partner, significant other or spouse. Would that person be okay with what they saw on that tape? If the answer is no then you need to make the choice that is in line with your integrity. The Videotape Test is an opportunity for you to quickly get a different perspective on your actions or behaviors to help make better choices.

There you have it. Several different tools and strategies to make better choices. If you make better choices you will create a better life. Ultimately everything comes down to the choices you make. How you respond or react to a situation is a choice. How you handle stress, anger, and depression are all choices. Your viewpoints on things that have happened in the past are choices. How you go about making your choices can change your world.

If you apply this in every avenue of your life you can change your life… you can change the lives of those around you. Especially if you share this information with your children

You have been given a new perspective on choices. You should now know that your life is a result of all the many choices you have made, good, bad and indifferent. You have been given tools to help you make better choices. You have new information such as choices and consequences, the Ten Second Rule, and the Videotape Test. I've given you this great information on how to help you make better choices, how you CHOOSE to use it is all up to you.

<u>LESSONS LEARNED</u>

1. Your choices got you where you are
2. You always have a choice whether it be good, bad or indifferent
3. Every choice has a consequence
4. The Ten Second Rule
5. Videotape Test

Chapter 8:
Seal The Deal

At this point you have a lot of information and been given many tools, tips, exercises and strategies to help you go from *now* to *wow*. Each is there to help you accomplish your dreams and goals and have the life you know in your heart is possible. You've thought about the goals you want to set for yourself. You've discovered your passion, made a plan, created ways to get past fear, and have a new way of thinking about choices and your beliefs. You may be thinking, "After all that, now what?" How would you like to have a simple three step process to significantly increase your odds of getting what you want? I have developed a process that can help you seal any deal, with yourself or with others. It can help you accomplish whatever you set out to do. It is amazing how something as simple as accountability can keep you honest and on the right track to achieving your goals.

This three step process is what I call the 3 C's to Success. And the three C's are:

Commit

Communicate

Create

As with most things, getting started is the hardest part. I have had many coaching clients tell me that very thing -- getting started is the hardest thing to do. Think about a time when you've started a workout program or new diet, getting started was the hardest part, wasn't it? This is exactly the reason why the first C is Commit. Commitment is the toughest of the 3 C's. It's where you figure out if what say you want really is what you want. Let's use the losing weight example again. You decide you want to be healthier, thinner, and leaner. Now it is time to make the commitment to do what is necessary to get there.

Perhaps your plan looks something like this:

Step One: Look into gym memberships, personal trainers and nutritionists.
Step Two: Research programs like Weight Watchers, Jenny Craig, Nutri-System etc to find the best fit for me.
Step Three: Determine realistic time frame to achieve my goal.
Step Four: Make decision on which program or plan I'm going to do.
Step Five: Choose a day to begin.
Step Six: Do it!

At step one you are looking into gyms to see if this is a good fit for you. Most likely, you will go online to do some research and ask around to friends and colleagues to see what other's experiences have been. Then you may go visit a gym or maybe even several of them – after all, there are so many too choose from. There's co-ed, women only, some that focus on cardio more than weights and others that specialize in group classes and yet at others you are just on your own. You go; you get more information and decide if it is the way you want to go. After you do your research and make a decision, you sign up. Which requires what? It requires you to sign a contract. Even if you don't use it you are still going to pay for it until your contract ends. You talk to a trainer because you are serious and want to do this right. They tell you all that's involved. The foods you need to eat, the weight training and cardiovascular exercise you will need to do and how often. They tell you how many calories you will be allowed to take in and how many you will need to burn to get to where you want to be.

At this point two things can happen. The first being, you step up and commit. Then what happens if you decide later you don't want to work out with the trainer anymore? That's ok, but you signed a contract and paid for your sessions and you are not likely going to get a refund. Or, two, you say, "Ya know what? I don't want to do all of this. I had no idea this is what it was going to take and I really don't want it that badly." If you say yes, I want to do this, then you sign on the dotted line. If you say no, you accept things the way they are and find a way to live with what you have until you are ready to do what is necessary to commit.

This example applies to almost anything in life. Let's say you want to buy a house. There are a lot of things involved and it's a significant commitment. Once you find the house you want, you put in an offer. Which is what? It's a contract, a written commitment. Once you sign, you can't simply come back a week later and say "nah, never mind I don't want it anymore." Well, you could, just not without consequences. If you did there could be some financial obligations for backing out after signing. The entire home buying process is exactly what we are talking about, one commitment after another. After the initial offer you have to agree to all the terms and get a mortgage – yet another commitment that comes with a contract.

How about marriage? So many people go into it without really being committed to it for life. Just look at the divorce rate and you'll know that's true. I know a lot of people who go into marriage thinking they can easily get out. Or, they think it will always be fun and happy and blissful. Even if you do think, or hope, that you will stay married until death do you part are you really "committed" to it? Are you really committed to putting up with the good, bad and the ugly to stay married to this person? Does marriage mean to you that you are committed to this person through thick and thin no matter what, forever and always? Have you thought about, and communicated to your partner about, how you will handle conflicts and make important decisions? Have you discussed those difficult things like how to avoid having an affair and what you will do if one of you does? Have you discussed how you will resolve arguments and conflicts? Do you agree on fighting fair, knowing each other's limits and when you need to stop and walk away to cool off and when you will come back and resolve the situation? Do you know how many children you want to have and how you will educate, discipline and expose them to religion? Will you both work full time and how will you handle it if one of you gets laid off?

There are a lot of things to consider when it comes to getting married. While it may seem as though I'm taking all the fun and love out of marriage, that is not my intention. However all of these things are important and need to be considered. Most if not all of these issues – and many, many more – will come up at some point in marriage. If you consider these things ahead of time and develop a plan you will have far fewer unhappy surprises. When you consider and discuss these things and have mutually committed to your decisions then you have a plan for a happy and successful marriage. Talking about the tough things, coming up with a plan and committing to it before there are insurmountable barriers between you, is the best thing you can do to create the life you want.

There would either be fewer marriages to begin with or fewer divorces if people viewed marriage as a lifetime commitment. This is exactly the approach I have taken. I decided that if I were to get married again I would think of it as a lifetime commitment that I cannot get out of for any reason. Did you or did someone you know think when they got married that there was no way out under any circumstances? I doubt it. Most of the time we close our eyes, hold our breath and hope for the best. With a divorce rate over 50 percent, clearly something needs to change.

Here is a perfect example from another client of mine who was divorced. According to him, the reason for the divorce was that his wife was very inhibited when it came to sex. She was not adventurous and was very closed off in the bedroom. He said if he had known ahead of time, he wouldn't have gotten married. I said. "Ok, let's look at this from an open and honest perspective. You are saying that you had no idea, no sign, no clue that this issue existed?" He responded with "NO! I had no idea." I said "You didn't have premarital sex?" He said "Yes we had sex before we were married but I thought it would change." At that moment he said "Well ok, I guess I had a little clue, but I thought things would change after we got married."

We continued to talk, but here's the gist: I said we generally have some sign or gut feeling telling us we really don't want to live with this one thing for the rest of our life. But we delude ourselves into thinking it will be ok, or it will change, or it will be different when we get married. Here's the problem: What you see is what you have and will continue to get. But we love this person and want to spend our lives with them and there are so many other good things. We say this one thing that isn't quite right doesn't really matter. If that "thing" truly doesn't matter, then fine. But if it does matter and it isn't likely to change, wouldn't you rather know that going in than have to figure it out five, ten, or twenty years and three children later?

What you should do from this point forward is ask yourself "if this 'thing' were to remain exactly as it is and will always be that way, am I willing to live with it forever?" Sometimes the answer will be yes. And sometimes it won't be.

Wouldn't you rather not get married knowing this "thing" is a deal breaker, than spend the next however many years trying to change the person, end up resenting them and later divorcing? All of these only lead to hurt feelings, lost time, wasted energy, spent money and possibly your children suffering as well. If there are deal breakers and you know it, recognize it and acknowledge it then you can confront them right away. If you decide that it is not what you want to live with then you can get out before much damage is done. Then, you are free to find the one you are truly meant to be with or you may find peace within yourself and live happily on your own.

We generally do know or have a hint of what we are getting ourselves into. *But,* we close our eyes to the things we don't like and think the situation, or the person, will change "after we get married." Yet it never fails that we are shocked when it doesn't – and then we want out. If we would think of what we are getting into when we marry as a lifetime commitment the divorce rate would, most likely, go down.

Here's a great example from my own life. Before I got married there were a couple things about my fiance that I knew would not work for me and that I considered deal breakers. He said they'd change "after we got married." Shockingly, they didn't. I remembered thinking that I knew these existed and I should have decided if I was ok with them and not expect them to change. As the old adage says, hindsight is 20/20. Getting a divorce was the hardest decision I have ever made. Yet, I can assure you I learned a valuable lesson and make better decisions now because of it. As valuable as that lesson was, it was a very difficult thing to go through. I often wonder if the only way to learn lessons is to go through the pain and suffering on our own. I honestly don't believe that's true. I have been a witness to many physically abusive relationships and I do not, and have not, needed to experience that for myself to know I don't want that in my life. You can learn lessons without the pain of experience. That is, if you choose to do so. A smart person learns from their own mistakes but a wise person learns from the mistakes of others.

You must think with your heart *and* your head. Just because you love someone doesn't mean you should marry them, or spend your life with them. You may love someone with all your heart but that doesn't change the fact that they are an abusive alcoholic. You need to think about the person you are going to marry and ask yourself some important questions. Is he or she a drinker? Do they smoke, have a temper, are they bad with money, messy, disorganized, abusive, bad in bed? Are you willing to live with any or all of these things? If a concern exists now, you aren't going to change it or them. So, you need to think thoroughly about what you are getting yourself into. You can't change other people. If a person wants to be different, it is up to them to change. Then they have to take the steps necessary to make that change – you can't do it for them.

Now, this example is kind of funny but when you buy a car you buy it with your heart and your head. You may like the way it feels and looks. You also may like that is safe and comfortable. Those are things that appeal to your heart and your mind because both are important. I personally think that every important decision in life should be made with your heart and your head. When you buy a car it should be affordable so you can pay for it and you should like the car when you drive it. When you buy a house you should like where it is, what it looks like, how it feels when you are inside it and be able to comfortably afford it. When you have children you should love the idea of being a parent, you should want the responsibility of being a parent, and be able to take on the expense of being a parent and providing for a child. Being a parent isn't just about loving your child, it is about providing for them and taking care of them as well. When making such a huge decision you should make it with your heart and your head.

If you purchase a car, and a week or so later decide you don't like it as much as you thought you did, you can't take it back. No buyer's remorse allowed. You signed a contract. You made a commitment to purchase that car and now it's yours. You can't just change your mind and return it. Similarly, if you get married and decide you don't like your husband or wife anymore you can't go back to their mother and say "I don't like this one anymore, can you take it back?" When you have children and realize it's a lot of hard work you can't put them back in and say "oops, this is harder than I thought. I'm not ready for this." But if you think your way through it and feel good about it then you are on your way to making a good, strong commitment.

Do you want to lose weight? Are you considering a new job or promotion? Are you buying a car or entering into a legal contract? Are you getting married or going to college? No matter what you are considering, first think about what is real or what is required. Think about all the things you know to exist and be honest about what you think and feel about all of them. Then decide if you want it. And that means you want ALL of it.

Tip #31- Be Committed

Exercise 8.1

1. Look at the goal you have set for yourself and write down all the things you will need to do in order to achieve your goal.
2. Next, write "Am I willing to commit to doing all the necessary things to achieve my goal?"
3. Write a contract and sign it.
4. To really seal the deal, get a couple of witnesses and have them sign it too.

Just remember, anytime you sign a contract you are making a commitment. Whatever you are doing, whatever choice you have to make, view it as a commitment and you will make better decisions and come out better in the end because you did. When you take this first C seriously and view all decisions and choices as a contract, then you will have completed the first step in sealing the deal.

This leads us to the second C in the 3 C's to Success – communication. The more you communicate your goal to yourself and to others the more likely you are to achieve it. Again, let's use the "losing weight" example. First off, the way you communicate with yourself is very important. The words you choose when you set goals is crucial to your success. I don't like to use the term "losing weight" because anytime you view something as a loss there is likely going to be some mental or emotional resistance. So, choose a goal that is stated in the positive. For example, if your ultimate goal is "losing weight", change it to something like, "I want to release some weight. I want to shed some fat. I want gain lean muscle mass, get slim, get healthy, strengthen my heart, extend my life." Can you see the difference?

Anytime you set a goal it is much better to add something rather than take something away. People usually think of dieting or weight loss as painful because they have to give up the foods they like or things they like to do. However, if you consider the good things you are gaining then you are one step closer to success. Instead of saying "I am giving up sugary or fatty foods," say, "I am only eating foods that are good for me. I'm only eating foods that are nutritionally sound."

Remember when you were a child and had something taken away from you as a punishment? Didn't you then just want it even more? That is most likely true in your adult life as well. If your doctor says you can't have red meat don't you instantly start to crave a nice big juicy steak? That's because we tend to want what we can't have. If you view the process of achieving your goal as a plus instead of a minus, you will enjoy the process and be much more likely to get what you want.

The way you communicate to yourself is extremely important but communicating to others is just as important and maybe even more so. Just think, if my goal is to get to my happy weight I am much more likely to accomplish it if I tell everyone around me what my goal is. Tell your family, friends and co-workers what you are working toward. Let's say you currently weigh 200 pounds and want to get to 175 or 150 or even 120. Tell everyone you work with that you are going to weigh 175 pounds by Christmas. Better yet, put up a sign in your cubical or office. You are a whole lot less likely to hit the Krispy Kremes in the break room on Friday if everyone around you knows what you are working towards. Surrounding yourself with reminders that will keep you on track is a great way to ensure accountability. Even if no one says anything, you know that you have told them and you know what they are thinking. Sometimes that is enough to keep you on the right track.

A great way to communicate with yourself, and to open the doors of communication to others, is to write your goal on sticky notes and place them all over your home, car etc. Seeing your goals posted all around you is a great reminder. Many people make New Year's

Resolutions, but few actually remember that resolution a month later, much less actually stick with it.

Writing down your goal, and putting it somewhere where you will see it every day is also a way of forcing you to share your goal with others. Most of the time, if people see you surrounded by sticky notes at work or at home, they'll ask what they're for. Sharing your goal and what you are working towards with others is yet another way to remind yourself and reinforce your goal.

The more senses you use to communicate the more likely you are to remember something. So, if I tell others I am using my voice and I am using my auditory sense as well. Then, I write it down so I am using my hands – the tactile sense, and then I read it, which is using my visual sense. I then envision myself being or having whatever it is that I am working towards while imagining what it would feel like to have it. That is using my feelings, and, as a result utilizing my kinesthetic sense. The more senses you use the more real it becomes.

Hopefully you now see the importance of communication as the second C to success. You must tell everyone around you in addition to yourself about your goal. I did this with the first book I wrote. For years and years I didn't tell anyone about the book I planned to write. I was teaching a class that had generally 50+ people in it. So at every class I started to share my goal. I had more than 50 people every weekend who knew what I was working toward. Then I got emails and phone calls all the time asking me how the book was coming along. Boy, did that keep me on track! How big of a schmuck did I look like if every time someone asked me how the book was coming and I said "what book?" or "uh yeah, it's on the back burner." I wouldn't have any credibility if I told people what to do but didn't do it myself. I told just about everyone I came in contact with what I was doing. The more people I told the more accountable I became. I didn't want to be seen as a liar or someone who thought big but never did. I wanted to do what I set out to do and the more people I told the more drive it gave me.

There are some things that you aren't going to want to tell everyone about because you don't want people to know what you are working on. For example, if you want to shed some pounds from your body that may not be something you want to share with a lot of people. However, I would ask you to ask yourself why that is? Do you not want to share your goal because you are afraid you won't achieve it? The more people you tell the more embarrassed you will be when you don't do what you said you were going to.

For example, let's say 175 pounds is your goal weight. You've told everyone you know what your goal is. It's posted at your desk and is the screen saver on your computer. Then, on Friday morning, when donuts are in the break room, everyone asks "How are you doing on the 175 pound goal?" I really don't think you are going to pop one of the Krispy Kremes into your mouth and say "GREAT!" Even if you were tempted to have one, you are likely a lot less inclined to now. The more people you tell the more people will keep you honest. You know darn good and well that you won't tell everyone you know about your mission to fit into the jeans you wore in high school and then in the same breath stuff a chocolate chip cookie into your mouth.

Now let's say you don't share your goal with anyone. Why would you not tell anyone what your goal is? Chances are you don't want anyone to notice when you don't reach it. Isn't that already setting yourself up for failure? I think so. If no one knows that you want to be 175 pounds by Christmas or to fit into those size eight jeans, then there's no harm in eating that 600 calorie donut with zero nutrition, because no one knew you weren't supposed to have it in the first place. But when there's a witness or two or three or more, you think before you do. You have others to hold you accountable or at least keep you honest.

That's why a workout buddy or something or someone to keep you honest and on track is a tremendous benefit. That is why people who go to Weight Watchers or Jenny Craig or have a trainer or a personal coach have higher success rates. There is always someone to answer to. Keeping your goal a secret is a well devised plan for failure.

Hundreds of thousands of people lost weight, or, in better terms, gained health, when they were on a program. But then they reach their goal and what do they do? They stop going to meetings or talking to their coach, right? Again, using the weight loss example, what almost always happens? You gain the weight back. You stop doing what worked. You stop having someone or a group of people keep you accountable. You no longer have anyone to answer to.

I learned this lesson very quickly when I had my first personal coach. Every time I'd set some objectives for my next week, I felt like a complete nincompoop when I didn't do them. And, boy, did she let me know how much I was degrading my own value or lessening my integrity anytime I failed to follow through on my weekly tasks. If I hadn't told her, or anyone else, what my intentions were, no one except for me would know I didn't do it. Chances are I'd "forget" what it was I was going to do in the first place. It's kind of like New Year's resolutions. You make a goal and write it down; only it's in some obscure place where no one (including you) can see it. Then you stumble on it months later only to realize you haven't even come close to achieving it. If you are serious about accomplishing anything, I suggest you get talking, but don't stop there. Talk, write, read, hear, see, and feel your goal.

Communication is really the key. Once you have committed, the next step is making it real by communicating with others and yourself. The commitment step is really all about you. *You* choosing and deciding that *you* are committed to doing what *you* need to do to reach this goal. Then the communication step is there to really lock it in and get you to tell others who can and will support you on your way to reaching this goal. I know you know someone to whom every time you tell something, it instantly becomes real. More real than ever before. Well, this is the first person you should tell. Then tell every single person who comes to mind what you are setting out to accomplish. The more you tell the more accountable you will become.

With the internet today this is easier to do than ever. You could post your goal on Twitter and have all of your followers support you and check in to see how you are doing. You could create a blog and publish daily postings to keep you on track. I met a woman, Kelly Jean, at a seminar once who did just that. She had a weight loss goal and she started a blog about it. This was her way of staying accountable. She was placing her daily progress on her blog for the whole world to see. What a great way to keep it real. Then she decided to step it up a notch. She created a fund raiser on her blog to raise money for America's Second Harvest Foodbank. You should use this idea with your goal. If you want to look at this example please visit her blog at www.jellyke ordpress.com. With more than 200 social media sites on the internet today you will no doubt be able to find one you like and post your goal.

Another great social media channel is Facebook. You can post on your wall what your goal is, or write it daily in "What's on Your Mind." How great would it be to post that you lost half a pound or a pound every day? Then, think of how great it would be to have all the virtual support as you are working towards your goal. This is a great way to share your goal with the world and ask for support. Ask for daily check ins or virtual   rs. Ask if anyone is interested is going on this journey with you. There's likely to be others that will have a goal similar to yours and discovering that you share the same goal may be just what they need to get started.

Remember to think outside the box when you are contemplating how to communicate your goal. The way you communicate does not necessarily have to be through conventional channels. You can talk, write, read, fax, email, post, blog and on and on and on. Be creative! Write down all the ways you can communicate your goal to increase your odds of accomplishing it.

Here's one more reason the second C, communicate, is important. To a lot of people their word means something. Have you ever had a flaky friend or someone who was always saying they were going to do something…and never does it? Has anyone ever told you they would help you move and then didn't show up on moving day? Did you ever trust that person to come through on anything ever again? Not likely. It doesn't take much for us to lose faith or not trust someone when they say they will do something and then don't follow through. In fact, it only takes one or two times for someone to flake out on us before we stop believing them. So then why are we okay with lying to ourselves time and time again? You know the answer. There is no one there to hold us accountable. You don't want to be one of those people do you? One that says a lot of stuff but never actually does it. You are a person of your word right? So step out and tell the world not what you are going to do but what you are already doing.

Are you going to talk or are you going to do? Do you say you're going to lose weight, quit smoking, stop drinking, get into shape? Do you do it? Words with no action are just words. Stop your talking and start doing. You have everything you need to get what you want. "I'm going to," can last a lifetime. Perhaps your intentions are good, but you just don't follow through. If you don't, you are lessening the value of your word and yourself. Don't just talk. Do.

Communicate what you want to yourself and others and communicate it in every form. You are far more likely to get what you want if you do.

Tip #32- Communicate! Share your goals with others.

Exercise 8.2

1. Write down your goal (yes, again).
2. Write down how you are going to communicate it.
3. Write a list of 25 people you are going to communicate this goal to.
4. Make a minimum of 5 phone calls and send 5 emails right now!
5. Continue to communicate the goal until you have reached all 25 people.

6. Ask anyone you want to touch base with you and ask how it is going every day.

7. Choose a social media site to communicate and/or start a blog.

The third C is really the easiest. After all, the hard work has already been done. If you committed and found a way to communicate, you are ready for C number three. Create. Believe it or not, this is the easy part. You have already done the hard work. You thought it through, you planned out what needed to be done. If you started with the first C then you have already done the research and know what it's going to take to get what you want. If you weren't up for the challenge and weren't willing to do what it took to get to your goal, then you would have stopped there. Therefore, by now you've committed and communicated. You've told everyone you know what you are doing – and notice I said "doing", not "going to do". You've written it down, you've signed a contract with yourself and you are surrounded by reminders of it every where you go. Now all you have to do is do it.

Create truly is the easiest step. Most of the time people are chomping at the bit through the other two steps to get to this so they can finally take action. That time has come. It is time to take action. The trick here is to keep your steps small and simple. Remember from Chapter 4, when we discussed planning? Break your steps down to things you can do every day. As excited as you are you don't want to get overwhelmed. Remember, if you dice things up into little simple bite size pieces you can do more than one a day if you want. But if you don't, then one tiny step at a time is still making progress toward your goal.

Commit, communicate, and create. It's as simple as 1,2,3 or C,C,C.

LESSONS LEARNED

1. Always research and think carefully about your goal
2. Sign a contract with yourself
3. Communicate your goal with yourself and others
4. Get a goal buddy

Chapter 9:
Knocking out the Negative

This chapter takes choices to a whole new level and reinforces that it can be empowering and enlightening when we take control and action on our own life. There are three main things you should take away from this chapter. Act or accept, can't versus won't, and reflection or projection to make negativity a thing of the past.

Every day, negative things happen to us. Is that fair? No. Is it part of reality? Yes. So, what can you do with the reality that you are given every day? In the previous chapters you learned all about choices. Act or Accept really is a deeper more powerful level of that concept. In the harshest of terms, one could say this chapter is all about put up or shut up. You have the choice to act or accept.

Talk, talk, talk. How often do you find yourself talking about something over and over and over again, that you can't or won't do anything about. Act or Accept is really a tool to use when you are dealing with a negative or difficult situation. This tool, when you use it, will assist and expedite the process to progress from negative to positive.

When you are facing a difficult situation I want you to ask yourself this question: Can I do anything about this? If you can, then ask yourself if you are willing to take action. If the answer to the latter is no, you are not willing to do anything, then you need to accept it for what it is and move on. If you cannot do anything about your situation – and I do mean can't not won't (but we will get into that later) – then the automatic answer is accept. Act or accept is a concept that, if you embrace it, can instantly change your emotional and mental disposition about any negative situation.

How many times have you had someone say or do something that was not nice or maybe even down right despicable to you? I think that has happened to most of us. But, let me ask you this, can you do anything about it? First, no matter what has happened to us in the past, it is in the past. There is nothing at all – zero, zip, zilch -- you can do about it now. Therefore, if you literally can't do anything about it, isn't is better to accept it for what it is and move on? Why continue to harp on it if it is in the past and there is nothing you can do to change it? The only thing you can change is your attitude or perspective.

You see, we can't change other people or their behavior. So if you don't like what someone says or does accept that you can't change other people and forget about it. You can use this concept and apply it to eliminate negativity in so many areas of your life.

Think about weight loss again. If you notice your clothes don't fit anymore and they are too tight and uncomfortable, before you grumble in your head or utter a word to yourself or to someone else about how unhappy you are with your size, ask yourself, am I willing to take action in order to make it be different? If the answer is no, then why waste your time thinking about it? Accept it for what it is and spend your time thinking about or doing something else. Something that is positive and productive. I mean, why grunt and grumble about something you are not going to do anything about? That is just a waste of time, energy and sanity -- plain and simple.

This philosophy can also apply to relationships. Here's an example: A friend of mine was engaged. She was calling me at least once a week with the same complaint about her fiancé. Now, I understand that all relationships have their own set of issues, and I also know that no relationship is perfect. But this dynamic, this same argument, came up at least a couple times a month, every month for a few years. She did not like that he drank as much and as often as he did. She also did not like that he would talk about his ex-wife as often as he did. Yet regardless of her complaints, his behavior continued.

Finally, one day I said, "you have been complaining about this situation for years. Sweetie, it isn't going to change because he doesn't want to change so let me ask you this: Are you willing to stay in this relationship if it were to stay the same or do you dislike it enough to get out?" She was silent. Then I said, "You have two choices here. You can stay in it and accept it for what it is because clearly he is not going to do anything different since he hasn't for the last five years. Or, you can say enough is enough and leave. It's that simple. Act and get out or accept and stay in."

A week later the relationship was over and she moved out. She later told me it was the moment I said "act or accept" that she realized there were not enough good things to outweigh the bad, and she was not going to accept it the way it was and got out. She decided to stop complaining about something and take action to change it.

You can also apply this to your professional life. I had a coaching client that I had been working with for at least two months. He was an entrepreneur who ran a small business and had a couple of employees who were not performing to his level of expectation. Silly things like running out of toilet paper or legal pads and other standard supplies were constantly happening. By his own admittance he agreed that he was part of the problem. He had never really set up policies and procedures or job descriptions for his employees. Up to this point they had always made it up as they went along.

This was fine in the beginning but as his office began to grow, a level of efficiency had become more and more necessary. The little mishaps and oversights were no longer acceptable. So, together we developed a game plan. We created a checklist of things that needed to be done each and every day. We wrote a policy and procedure manual, job description and expectations, time sheets, etc.

Then we came up with a roll out date for implementation. The date was set for the day before our next coaching call when he was having his regular weekly office meeting. I was excited to hear how the meeting went because I knew this was really going to increase his efficiency and productivity. When he called on the day of his appointment, he didn't sound half as excited as I had anticipated. I asked, "How did the meeting go with all the new things you are implementing?" His response was less than stellar. I got something along the lines of "oh, yeah that. Uh, hhmm. Well we kind of went off in a couple of other directions and I didn't have the chance to roll them out."

We did a little of the why not and what happened, excuse, accountability, excuse, accountability and so on. Ultimately, we determined that he would roll out his new plan the following week.

Three weeks later and three meetings with his staff later, he had done none of them. The next time he complained I said, "I'm sorry you are having these issues. However, we came up with several solutions but you're not applying them. You are obviously getting more out of complaining because you *could* fix the problem but you *choose* not to. Therefore, I am no longer going to listen. You want to vent about the problem and do not want to solve it. You have two choices, you can act or accept. You can accept the situation for what it is, but then you really should not complain about it anymore because if you accept it there would be nothing to complain about. It is what it is. Then you can take all that time and energy you are using and apply it to something much more productive. The other alternative is to Act. Take ACTION. Do something about what you are complaining about. You have the tools, use them."

I know this sounds harsh but it is completely true. Does talking about something and not taking action make it different? No. The same thing happened to me when I was getting chubby and my clothes weren't fitting. I was complaining about my clothes not fitting and not liking how I looked in the mirror. I was complaining about it but not doing anything to change it. When I found myself standing in the middle of the kitchen eating brown sugar straight from the box, I discovered the act or accept concept.

I asked myself what I wanted more: to eat anything I want whenever I want or to feel healthy and comfortable in my clothes. Mind you, this was my decision. No one would have said I was "fat" because I was fortunate enough to gain weight throughout my entire body not just in one area. So it wasn't really noticeable to others that I had put on some weight. However, I knew when I couldn't close the button on my pants, or get the skirt I wanted to wear over my hips that I wasn't in the shape I wanted to be in. I realized at that moment I had a choice. I could accept my body for what it was, or I could take some action to change it.

Tip #33- Act or Accept

Exercise 9.1

1. Write down what you find yourself complaining about.
2. Are you complaining just to have something to talk about or are you complaining because you want something different?
3. If you do want something different are you willing to act and do something starting right now?
4. If you chose act, then write a goal and start a plan, and start right now. No reason for delay.
5. If you chose accept, write down on a piece of paper "I choose to accept _____. From this point forward I am free of any negative thoughts or feelings about it." Then burn the page and move on.

This exercise is extremely important because you really need to know if you are willing to do something to change what you are complaining about. If you don't want to change the situation, that's fine. Or, if you do want to change the situation but you don't want to do the work to make it change, that's okay too. Either way, you need to accept. With no action there is only one other choice and that choice is to accept. Well, I suppose there is one other choice and that would be to keep everything the same and continue to be miserable, complaining about the same things. Why would you want to do that? If you are reading this book you are looking to make a change and I know you are not going to stay in the same situation and do nothing. You are either going to accept the situation the way it is or you are going to act and do something to change it.

Money and finances are a common complaint with many people. I hear all the time the typical complaints of "I don't have enough money" or "I don't make enough money" or "I spend too much money." I once had someone tell me that she needed to stop spending so much money. I said "if it were me, I would just go make more. That's a lot more fun than cutting back." This girl almost fell off her chair when I said that. She was amazed at such a different and positive approach. Shortly thereafter she took on a little side job, just a couple of hours a week, that allowed her to maintain her spending habits but not feel the financial crunch. This allowed her to be happy and relax because she wasn't concerned about the money she was spending every time she bought something she wanted.

A woman I know has been unhappy with her job and her boss and everything else about her current work for some time. Her skills are not being utilized to the fullest of her abilities or interests. After months of discussing this, I decided to approach her with some hard and fast "coaching" questions. Things like, what would you like to be doing if you weren't doing this job? What role do you see yourself in? What kind of money would you like to make? What would be the ideal company to work for? She was answering the questions pretty quickly and easily so I knew these were things she had thought about. She had been to many of my seminars and had done the thinking work but had yet to apply the doing work. The coach in me started to jump in and ask what was stopping her from taking action.

With a tear, the truth about fear came out. Fear. She was afraid of failing. She was afraid of all the worldly "what if's." What if I try and fail?

What if I'm not good at what I think I want to do? What if I can't make it? The question that really made her take action was this: I said, "Let's just say that you did embark on this new adventure and you did fail, or you realized this isn't what you wanted after all. Would that be so bad? Wouldn't that enable you to move on and put this one behind you so you can find something that you do want and love?" Literally, the next day, we met to work on her resume and cover letter which has been sent out to several possible companies and the interview process has begun. Since then, she doesn't complain about her existing work anymore because she knows there's an end in sight and a new beginning to follow.

This woman chose to act and not accept her situation as it was. She realized she was complaining about a situation that she could change if she took the action to do so. Now it's time for you to work on a situation you have been dealing with. Follow along and do the next exercise. These questions are in different groups where most people are looking for change. Money/career, physical, relationships, and education.

Tip #34- Accept the situation you are in or do the work to change it.

Exercise 9.2 money/career

1. How much money do I want to make?
2. What would I do with the money I made?
3. What job would I love or dream to have?
4. How much would it pay?
5. What would be the perks?
6. Why do I want it?

Exercise 9.3 physical

1. What about my body do I want to change?
2. Why do I want to change it?
3. How much do I want to weigh?
4. What size do I want to be?

5. How do I want to feel?
6. Do I want to change for me or for someone else?
7. If I had my dream body, how would I feel?

Exercise 9.4 relationships

1. What am I looking for in a relationship?
2. Why do I want to be in a relationship?
3. What would the ideal relationship look like?
4. What would the ideal relationship feel like?
5. How would I be in a relationship?
6. How would my partner be in a relationship?
7. What characteristics am I looking for in a partner?
8. What does your ideal partner do for work?
9. What does your ideal partner do for fun?
10. Where does the type of man/woman I am looking for go?
11. Where can I go, what can I do, to meet my ideal mate?

Exercise 9.5 education

1. What is my current level of education?
2. What do I want my level of education to be?
3. Why do I want a higher level of education?
4. What is my area of interest?
5. Which schools am I interested in?
6. Do I want a degree, certification, etc?
7. How long do I expect it to take to achieve this?
8. Am I willing to do what is necessary?
9. What do I have to do to start working towards this today?

This exercise will allow you to open up your mind and see the life you want. You may come up with more or better questions. Ask yourself, and answer, everything that comes to mind. This is your opportunity to find out if you really do want what you say you want. Then you will be able to determine if you are going to act or accept.

Perhaps you are on the other side of the spectrum. Maybe you're a minimalist. You don't want or need much. The question for you would be, are you doing a job that you like and enjoy? I know so many people that don't want a lot of money, but they also aren't happy. Many times people aren't happy because they're doing a job they don't like. Day in and day out they aren't doing something they like and enjoy. How would you like to spend your time doing what you love and living the life you want? I think that would be the best of both worlds.

I know probably better than anyone what it's like to have the golden handcuffs on. I had a job where I made six, mid six, high six and then seven figures. How do you leave a job that pays you money that allows a lifestyle better than you could have ever imagined? And one that you enjoy, to boot! I loved my lifestyle. I was happy and comfortable. But, and it's a big but, I didn't enjoy what I was doing, at least not 10 years later. So many people told me that I couldn't have my cake and eat it too. Do you realize what a silly saying that is? Why have cake if you can't eat it? Doesn't that completely defeat the purpose of having the cake? I didn't understand why I couldn't break the rules. Besides, they weren't my rules. I didn't have anything to do with setting them up. Who said you have to do a job you don't like to provide you with the lifestyle you want? Who said if you do the job you love you have to be broke? So I decided to write my own set of rules. And you can too. This is your next exercise, write your own rules about the life you want. Be big, be specific, no boundaries, no holds barred. Just you and your imagination. Let 'er rip!

Tip #35- Write your own rules

Exercise 9.6

1. Write your own rules.
2. What do you want out of your life?
3. What do you want to put into life?

4. What kind of career, health, relationship, education, etc do you want?

5. Be specific, be clear and be courageous. Step out of the box and set the stage for the life you want.

Now you get to decide. Are you going to act or accept? Are you going to take some action, make a plan and take the steps necessary to get what you want? Or, after looking over all the answers to your exercises are you thinking you are ok with the situation the way it is and are going to accept it for what it is and spend your complaining time and energy in better ways?

Thus far, we have discussed Act or Accept, this leads us to Can't versus Won't. Many times we are faced with negative things that we can't do anything about. Other times we are faced with things that we can do something about, but choose not to, or, rather won't do something about. I think a lot of people get caught up in can't. To me, can't means that you are physically not able to do something. I encourage you to take this literally. For instance, a quadriplegic can't walk. It is physically not possible for one to stand up and walk. You can't go back in time. Literally, as yet at least, it is not possible for one to go back in time and do something over. I'm 5'4" tall. I can't make myself be 5'6" tall, it physically isn't possible. These are all examples of can't.

Won't, however, is entirely a different story. Won't means you are physically capable of doing something, but you choose to not take action. How many times do you say "I can't say no?" When in truth you can say no, you are physically capable of saying the word no. It may be difficult for you to say no for whatever reason but you can say no. You simply need to make the effort to say it. Trust me, I know what this one is like. I agree to things all the time because I hate to disappoint people. However, there comes a time when you need to do what is right for you. Sometimes saying no is difficult but it can be done.

As an example, I was working with a coaching client who was a loan officer in the mortgage business. This woman had weekly assignments and one of them was to go find real estate agents to work with. A few weeks of excuses for not doing this passed and the point of no return came. I asked her what the problem was. "Why are you not going into these offices?" Her response was, and I'm paraphrasing, "I just can't. It's too intimidating. I'm lacking in self confidence. My parents were divorced when I was two, I didn't see my dad much, my mother always told me I wouldn't amount to anything. So I pretty much felt rejected by both my parents and that has been something I have dealt with my entire life."

I certainly understood and empathized. However, I asked her if she physically couldn't walk to the door, extend her arm and grab the knob, open the door and walk in? Naturally, her answer was, "Well, yes I could do that." I let her know that there is a big difference between "can't" and "won't." "Can't" means, "it is not physically possible." "Won't" means, "you are physically capable but choose not to." After considering this for a moment, she reluctantly agreed.

I then asked if there was any bodily harm that could occur from her walking in and talking to real estate agents. Of course the answer was no. Then I asked, "Is there any possibility that you could die from talking to them?" Again, the answer was, "No" "So," I asked, "what is the worst thing that could happen?" She said, "They could tell me to get out of their office and not waste their time." I said, "Is that all?" Her answer was "Yes." I asked her if, in reality, she was saying that she can't talk to these people or that she won't? Her answer was obviously won't and from that moment on, she took action and starting making the calls she needed to and her business exploded.

Another example of this is in conflicts or break ups. It is so hard to tell someone that you are no longer in love with them or that you don't have the same feelings for them as they do for you. Most people have been in the situation where someone is interested in you but you do not have the same feelings for them. I had an experience several years ago where I was dating someone and over six weeks he had fallen in love with me, but I didn't have the same feelings. I knew it was time for me to communicate what was going on in my heart and mind. That is a tough conversation to have! I could have made all the excuses in the world to not see him, not call him back and let him figure it out, but I didn't want to be "that" person. I don't like it when men do that to me and I certainly did not want to do that to someone else. I chose to meet this man face to face and tell him I was sorry but I didn't have romantic feelings for him. That was one of the toughest conversations I have ever had to have and it was not well received. He was hurt and upset but later respected and appreciated my honesty.

He came back a few weeks later and said he was grateful that I let him go and was honest about it early on so he didn't waste anymore time on someone who didn't love him back. No one wants to give that speech and no one wants to get it. However, I believed in my heart that it was best to be honest and not lead him on to think something more was going to come of our relationship. Many would say "I can't tell him I'm not interested." Yes you "can." Truth be known, you don't want to because it's a difficult conversation to have and who wants to have a difficult conversation or confrontation? It can be done you just have to choose to do the things that are difficult.

It seems as if people, at least in the US, have decided to start using "can't" in place of "I could but it would be too hard." I can't say no. Yes you can it's just easier not to. How many times have you said yes to something you didn't really want to do but did it anyway and then resented it? That's likely happened to many of us. It is much easier to say yes and wish you hadn't than say no to begin with. After all, if you say yes and you did what was best for someone else then you get to be the martyr right?

Here's the problem when you say can't: you are giving the responsibility to someone or something else as if you don't have a choice. But you do have a choice. Somehow it has just become so easy to say can't. By taking the responsible and accountable approach you will be liberating and empowering yourself to take charge of your life. When someone asks you to do something and you have a hard time saying no, say "let me check my calendar" instead. Think it through and choose for yourself if you want to do it. Just by making that a new habit you will instantly take on less. When you call back you will have a reason why you are not able or do not want to do what they asked.

Something came to my attention recently -- the use of can't in an instance of adultery. A woman was saying that she "could not" ever have an affair. I said "sure you could. You are physically capable of having extra marital sex." She said, "No, I could not do it. I literally could not do it." After asking why she responded with, "It just is not in my make up. It goes against everything I stand for and I would never be able to live with myself."

Again I found this interesting because she used the word can't. She did have sex with her husband so she was capable of having sex, but because her morals and integrity would prevent her from having sex outside the marriage, she said she couldn't. Why is that? Why is it easier for us to say we can't as if it is out of our control when it is completely in our control? I think it is much more powerful to say I would not have an affair because I would choose not to. I choose to keep my integrity and still be able to look myself in the mirror. Why would we want to lessen the importance or value of our choices. Why would we want to lessen our integrity? Saying that we can't makes it seem as if we have no choice in the matter and yet the choice is all ours. We should encourage that. We should embrace when we have such strong integrity that it prevents us from wrong doing. That is much more powerful than the passive, sloughing it off as if it's not a big deal and our minds, choices, and integrity had nothing to do with it.

This is something that should be reinforced to our youth and young children today: step up and make good choices and decisions and to be proud of when we make ones that represent strong integrity and good character. That is what will change the world and the people in it. When we all step up and take responsibility for our actions, good, bad and indifferent. When we take responsibility and are accountable for our actions then we will make a difference in our lives and in the lives of those around us.

The next exercise is designed to increase your awareness of the words you use and to see if you choose words that empower or weaken your integrity and choices.

Tip #36- Be responsible for yourself and your situation.

<u>**Exercise 9.7**</u>

1. For one day, keep track of how many times you say can't and the context in which you say it.
2. At the end of the day, look back at the number of times you said it and ask if it really was can't or was it won't.
3. If you determine that it really was can't, ask if you were physically not able, or was it a choice you were making?

By doing this exercise you should become aware of what you are saying and how the words we use can lift us up or break us down. Start to use words and communicate in a way that increases your value and validates your integrity. I'm pretty sure you will be amazed at how often you say can't when you really mean won't. This is a great way to start empowering yourself.

The last item in Knocking Out the Negative is something that just about every person has faced at least once in their life. Stress. Stress is a terrible thing to feel and it strips us of those precious moments of time and sanity when we are feeling it. However, stress is caused by one of two things: reflection or projection.

Many times when we are worried, stressed out or just stuck in the negative we are thinking about things that have already happened (reflection) or things we anticipate will happen (projection). Neither one of those has anything to do with this present moment. If you are feeling stress you are not in the now. You are in the future or in the past. Nothing can be wrong in any given second. Every second in and of itself is perfect. Not being in the moment is what causes stress.

If you are thinking about something that has already happened that has you stressed or angry, you are reflecting. Reflection is only dwelling on the past. It is history. It is over and done with. You are where you are now and that is what you need to focus on.

If you are thinking about something that has not yet happened, something you are concerned might happen then you are projecting. If it has not occurred yet and is not happening now then you are thinking about the future. It does not exist yet. How many times have you lost sleep or been grumpy or angry projecting into the future to what may or may not happen? If such and such is there I will say or do this. If I get home and the house is a mess I will be so mad. I need to talk to my husband or wife about this situation, and if they say this, that or the other I am going to wring their neck. I want to ask my boss for a raise or tell them I'm quitting, what are they going to say? What if they say this, what if they say that? What if, what if, what if. Why? Why do this to yourself? There is no good that can or will come of it.

How often did the thing you spent hours thinking and fussing and fuming over, not happen? All you can do is control you. Your actions and reactions. You can start to get control of your mental and emotional well being by staying in the moment.

Here is an exercise to help you work through stress when you are feeling it. Over time it will become a habit and you will find that you no longer have to deal with stress. There is, however, a caveat to this tool. You must use it. If you walk away from this book and don't apply this tool, or any of these tools for that matter, they will not work. Just being exposed to this information is not enough to make it happen. You have to do the work and apply the tools and information to make a difference.

I know we all want the easy solution, the quick fix. We want the magic pill that is going to make us instantly thinner. We want all of our problems to miraculously disappear with the wave of a wand with no effort of our own. We want Prince Charming or Cinderella to appear without us having to kiss any frogs or put ourselves out there. Unfortunately it doesn't happen that way.

If you want to make change in your life and have less stress, do this exercise.

Tip #37- Stay in the moment

Exercise 9.8

1. When you are stressed out ask yourself "am I in the present moment?"
2. Am I projecting or reflecting?
3. Label the thing that is on your mind and write next to it Past, Present, or Future.
4. Determine which one it is and circle it.
5. Take a slow breath in and out and say I release the past or I release the future.
6. Now ask yourself, "what do I do right now?"

There are several examples that flood into my mind of times I felt and defeated stress. I enjoy giving personal examples and not just those of people I have interviewed or coached because I want you to know and really feel that I am not preaching from an ivory tower. I walk my walk and talk my talk. These are not just made up stories or things I have heard. I know and understand what you are going through. I have been there and I can honestly share with you, through experience, the things that have allowed me to move past these defeating behaviors.

You may have heard that there are four main stressors people have the most difficult time dealing with. These are: death, divorce, moving and job change. I have been through every last one of them, more than once. I don't think any one is easier than any other. They are all difficult, but they are all different. You have already read my story of moving from California to New York completely on my own. If I didn't know what I know now, I don't think I could have done it. I would have changed my mind halfway through. Knowing how to handle stress and practicing what I preach, made it easier. There was a lot to do and it was a lot to handle but I stayed in the moment and never once lost sleep due to stress.

There were several times during the house selling, or packing, or shipping moments when I would feel myself getting stressed. Thoughts of this and that were rolling around in my head and several times I had to remind myself to practice what I preach. I was projecting. Almost always, I realized I was thinking of all the things that needed to be done and I would start to feel overwhelmed. At that moment I would first say "stop" out loud. I realized I was thinking into the future about how I was going to get it all done. Then I would take one long deep breath in and release it. Then I would grab a pen and paper (which I have made a habit to always have with me at every moment) and write down what I needed to do. Writing everything down, just that by itself, took nearly every ounce of stress away. I wasn't going to forget anything. It was on paper not just in my head. That kept me present and I moved 3000 miles away, 100% on my own with next to no stress.

Death is probably the most difficult. I had one of my best friends die in 2008 and it was one of the most devastating moments of my life. I quickly realized so much of what was causing my upset was reflection or projection. Did I say I love you that last time we spoke? Did he know I loved him even if I didn't say it? How could I not have known about this? What could I have done to prevent it? Am I partially responsible? How will I live without him? How does life go on?

Look at all those questions. What do you see? Do you realize that every last one is about the past or the future? If I didn't say I love you, if he didn't know, what can I do about that now? Nothing. I can't bring him back from the dead and redo it. Could I have prevented it? I don't know. I don't think so, but truthfully it doesn't matter now because even if I could have, I can't change history. I can't go back in time and change what happened.

Of course, once you get past the fact that you can't change history, you have to deal with the future. How are you going to live without them? How does life go on? What am I going to do? In the end the real answer is, one moment at a time. If you project into the future you will only cause yourself stress. By staying in the moment, by staying present, there is no sadness, no worry, no loneliness.

One day when I was crying and thinking of my friend who was no longer here I wondered, "How do I deal with this? What do I do?" Instantly, again, I realized I was projecting. I wrote out the question on a piece of paper, "What do I do now?" Then I got present. I sat quietly and just breathed. I felt myself relaxing. My mind stopped wandering and after a few minutes I just sat in the quiet. The next moment four letters came into my head. FFAD. My eyes shot open and I wrote them down. Then I said out loud, "What's a FFAD?" I again got present, closed my eyes and breathed. A moment later the answer came. Friends Fight Against Drugs. All of a sudden I knew what I was supposed to do: start a charity to help friends fight against drugs.

Projecting into the future is what causes stress. You can't find answers to the problems of today by projecting into tomorrow. The problem doesn't exist tomorrow, the problem exists now. Answers will come to you now, if you get into the now. There is just the moment. At the end of the day, you can't change history and the future doesn't exist. Stress lies in the future and in the past, peace lies in the present.

So what do you do to stay in the moment and not reflect or project? First thing is to give yourself a code word. Something that will make you get present. Maybe it's screaming STOP at the top of your lungs. Someone once told me that when I felt he was not listening to me and we were going off on some tangent to say "follow the yellow brick road" and that would snap him back into the moment. Making a plan is the very best way to get present. So often we get caught up in the fuss that we lose ourselves and forget that we have tools that we can use. Again, the very first step is awareness. Be aware and use your tools.

You can always find a good distraction from what is bothering you to help get you back in the moment. You can stop what you are doing and take a deep breath. You can write or simply name all the things you are grateful for. You can read a book or watch a movie. These are great escapes that can almost instantly stop the insanity and get you back into the moment.

The best thing you can do for yourself is to be aware of when you are stressed and be willing to change it. Then ask yourself if you are thinking of the past or the future. Do whatever works best for you to get in the moment. Remember to breathe and stay in the moment as much as you can. The second you follow these steps you will instantly feel less stress.

When it comes to knocking out the negative, you have many new tools in your toolbox. Act or accept. Look at your situation, whatever it may be and decide if you are going to take action or accept it for what it is. Then think of the words you use. Do you say can't when you really mean won't. Use this as a time to empower yourself and your integrity to make good strong choices that show who you are and what you are made of. Last but not least, when you are feeling stressed as we all do, look a little deeper. Discover if you are reflecting or projecting. As soon as you figure it out, stop, and get into the now. After all, it's only this one moment of time that matters.

LESSONS LEARNED

1. How to change your life by acting on or accepting your current situation.
2. The questions to ask to determine if you should act or accept.
3. How to get past limiting beliefs and excuses to not take action by understanding the difference between can't and won't.
4. How to take action when you change your words from can't to won't.
5. How to reduce stress by staying in the moment using the reflection or projection concept.
6. How to accept things in the present moment to eliminate negativity.

Chapter 10:
Putting off Procrastination

I'm guessing this isn't the first self help book you've read. Have you applied what you have learned from all the others? Some do, some don't. So let me ask you. Why are you procrastinating? What's the delay? Why have you not started before? Why are you hesitating in starting now?

There was a time in my life that I procrastinated too. I seemed to put everything off. One day I realized I was just delaying the pain. Once upon a time I was getting audited by the IRS and boy was that a painful experience. I looked at the box of documents that I needed to sort through day after day after day. Not only was it an eye sore having this box in the middle of the floor but it was causing me more and more pain by delaying the inevitable. It needed to get done and it wasn't going to be easier tomorrow or the next day. So I sat down and just did it. And boy did I feel a huge sense of relief when it was over.

It just seems that everything that needs to get done for whatever reason turns out much better when it is handled timely as opposed to not. When I was in the sales business bad news fast was often better than good news that took a long time to get. And it was certainly better than bad news that took a long time. Isn't that the case in most situations? Same philosophy applies to dating. If you and someone are not going to turn out to be something special isn't it better to know that up front or early on than waiting and waiting for the same news just weeks and weeks down the road? I suppose it is somewhat like ripping off the band-aid quickly and all at once. But the good news is the pain is over much quicker that way.

Now I do believe that all things happen for a reason, but I also think that when we are presented with an opportunity it is up to us to take action. Many times the rewards would have been better or the consequences less severe if action would have been taken sooner. I honestly can not think of a time when putting something off had better results than taking action would have. Does your car get better or worse when you delay getting the check engine light checked? Does your health get better when you put off taking care of yourself? Do your lungs get better when you put off quitting smoking? Can you think of anything that gets better when you put off doing what needs done?

I'm sure you have things you don't like to do. Most people don't like doing paperwork on anything and will avoid it like the plague. I used to hate to do reports and spreadsheets but let me tell you I like it a whole lot more where they're done. Same goes for bills. I get one in the mail, I pay it and it goes back in the mail the same day. No clutter, no fuss.

This goes for anything and everything. I no longer delay anything I need to do. Anything that needs to get done, it goes on my accomplishment list and it gets... accomplished. And let me tell you I am a much more relaxed and almost stress free all day everyday because I rarely have anything hanging over my head. I just deal with it when it comes up. Delaying the inevitable only prolongs the pain and that to me is worse than just getting it over with. Think about what you are delaying and then think about why. As soon as you become aware of what is holding you back you can work with it and let it go. It's almost like going to a doctor for something that is ailing you. Don't you just hate not feeling good day after day and when you go to the doctor they have to do test after test after test. It's so frustrating and you just want to throw your hands in the air and say enough already! Just figure out what's wrong so I can deal with it.

So, why do we procrastinate? Let me tell you I couldn't figure out for the longest time what my problem was. Why was I not doing what I knew needed to be done? I mean really. In my head I knew I was just delaying the inevitable and what I was doing made no sense whatsoever. Why put off and put off when you know you need to do something? It just makes no sense at all. I figured if I could make it make sense then maybe I would stop doing it. Finally, I did some reading and research on why humans procrastinate. Here is what I found.

There are five main reasons why people procrastinate — Anxiety, Failure, Success, Perfectionism or Resistance. Basically it all comes down to fear. However, many people perceive fear and procrastination differently. Therefore, we are going to shed some light on each of the reasons people procrastinate and put off the things they need to do.

Anxiety. Do you have anxiety about what needs to be done and that is why you are putting it off? Typically anxiety is directly related to the beginning or the ending of a task. That's usually because what needs to be done, seems overwhelming or frightening. How many times do you put off doing your taxes? Is that because the actual process of doing your taxes is too challenging or too difficult? Another good example is situations like having an elderly parent knowing there are certain things that need to be dealt with and you really don't want to face it. It's something you'd rather push back to the dark corners of your closet and not deal with. But rarely, does this work in our favor.

Failure. Another reason people procrastinate. Are you not doing what you know you should do because you expect you may fail? Is it safer and easier to say you didn't get what you want because you didn't try? What's the alternative? To say you didn't get what you want because you did try but failed? I believe that it's better to have tried and failed than to never have tried at all. Don't you waste more mental energy thinking about doing something as opposed to just doing it?

Success. Yet another reason people procrastinate. Many will not do what they are capable of doing because they know it will result in success. Success is heavy and carries a responsibility with it. Are you nervous or unsure about the responsibilities you will have if you reach your goal? Is it the reason you aren't taking action?

Perfectionist. Perfectionists tend to take no action if they can't do it perfectly. I have seen people who have absolutely disaster-ous home improvement projects both inside and outside that haven't been finished. So the inside of their kitchen may be half ripped out and not functioning but they won't do anything to fix it until they have the plans just perfect, down to every last detail. This makes no sense to me. Why would you rather live in complete and total chaos than make the situation decent and livable?

Resistance. Yet one more reason people put off what needs to done. If you are being required to do something that you do not want to do or do not see the value in, you may put it off until the very last possible moment or permanently if you can get away with it. Many times with school or work you have to do things you really don't want to do. You have to take prerequisite classes for school or you have to sit through an HR presentation at work even though you have been there for 10 + years and never had an HR problem. You don't want to do any of these things. They are annoying nagging things you need to do, but you put them off because there are plenty of things you want to do that are far more appealing.

The most common denominator here is fear. If you read chapter five you should know how to kick your fear in the rear. Putting things off or procrastinating is only going to make matters worse. If there are consequences to something, those consequences are still going to be there when you finally get around to facing them, and they will likely get worse the longer you put it off. Ask yourself, "What am I afraid of," and then deal with it. Many times, if not always, things are worse in our head than reality ever turns out to be. Just be honest and admit the fear, deal with it, get past it and step up and live your life NOW!!!

If something doesn't work out the way you want it to, it's ok, you can now move on to something else.

Tip #38- Procrastinate no more!

Exercise 10.1

1. Write down something you have wanted or needed to get done, but haven't taken action on.
2. Ask yourself why? Then write it down.
3. Look over the main reasons for procrastinating and find the one that best fits you.
4. Write down the best outcome and the worst outcome.
5. Now ask yourself, by putting it off are you helping or hurting yourself.

How often have you put something off for one reason or another? The thing is, if you got a positive result, you only delayed receiving the positive by procrastinating. You could have had it sooner if you would have just taken action. If you had a negative result you prolonged the pain and made it last longer than necessary. The anticipation of the pain is generally as bad if not worse than the pain itself. Had you taken action you would have been past the pain and on the road to recovery or happiness.

Have you ever had to end a relationship with someone? Just the thought of having the conversation would give you the cold sweats. You know you need to get this over with but oh how you hate confrontation and things like organizing your sock drawer or sticking sharp needles in your eye seems far more appealing and less painful. We've all been there. Think back to a time when you knew you had to have an uncomfortable conversation, and you put it off and put it off. Now think about the end result. Didn't you feel much better after it was done? Weren't you able to breath a sigh of relief when it was over? Better yet, did you walk away thinking "that wasn't as bad as I thought it was going to be and why did I wait so long to deal with it."

I have had those times and I have heard many stories from my coaching clients who have been dreading dealing with something and when they finally did it, it was so much easier than they anticipated. Again, good or bad why prolong the inevitable?

Have you ever had a wonderful idea that you just knew in your gut would be a huge success if you did it? Perhaps you thought about it for a little while but ultimately didn't do anything. Then, shortly thereafter as you were walking or driving down the street you saw that someone else did what you only thought about. If only you had taken action that multi gazillion dollar idea would have been yours, and you would be the multi gazillionaire. How many times have you said "I wish I would have done this sooner"? However, have you ever said "I wish I would have put blank off"? I don't think I have ever heard myself or anyone else say that. What does that tell you? It tells me that no good comes of procrastinating.

Tip #39- Take action now

Exercise10.2

1. Look at the last exercise, what are you delaying doing?
2. Do you really want it?
3. To check in and see if you do really want it, write down 20 reasons why you want what you say you want.
4. Look over your 20 reasons and ask again, do I really want this?
5. If your answer is yes, write a plan right now with the steps you are going to take to get it.

Money and finances are areas where people put off doing what they need or should do to create a secure financial future. Do you know you should open an IRA or other investment plan but just don't seem to get around to it? Seriously, would it take that much time to do the research? Is it really so overwhelming that you simply cannot deal with it? I doubt it. So why are you procrastinating? My guess is that you are afraid of what you will find. What you will find is that if you don't do something and do something now that you will never be able to retire because you won't be able to afford to. Does putting that realization off make the outcome any better? NO! But if you were to do it and do it now, you would be in a much, much, MUCH better place. More importantly if you would have done this sooner you would have been in an even better place. If you take action now you could still secure a very comfortable, if not extraordinary financial future. If you don't you are quite possibly prolonging your pain.

Same thing goes for making more money now. I can't tell you how many times I thought about how I would like to make more money than I did and all the things it would allow me to do, and have and give, when I was manicuring. Or, even when I was a phlebotomist, or in retail or a secretary. If I made more money, I could go on this trip, or buy this or that, or donate to charity and really make a difference. If only…

What's up with that?!? What was I thinking? Was money just going to fall out of the sky and change my life? I suppose it could but I think getting struck by lightening was more likely. Didn't I say earlier that winning the lottery is not a good or smart financial plan? If you want to make more money, then come up with a plan, and do it. Waiting around for the money gods to deliver a check to your door is just crazy.

If you want more money now, or later, or both then get off your duff, stop procrastinating and make a plan.

Tip #40- Hoping and wishing is not a good financial plan.

Exercise10.3

1. Write down how much money you want. Both now and later. How much do you need or want to live the life you desire?
2. Write down the jobs that pay the amount you want to make. Don't just think about "jobs" you can do. Think about all the WAYS you can make it. Perhaps just a job won't cut it.

3. Write down your step by step plan so you can get it.

No matter where you are in your life now, no matter what you are putting off, just do it. Face the fear, face the facts of your situation and then seize the day to make it better. Start now! It's easy when you have a plan.

LESSONS LEARNED

1. Putting things off only prolongs stress, or makes it worse.
2. Fear is the main reason for procrastination – so know your fears and beat them.
3. Taking action actually sets you on the road to recovery.
4. Things are usually not as bad as we think they are before we actually deal with them.
5. Anyone can increase their income if they just stop putting it off.

Chapter 11:
Wrap it Up

As the title suggests this chapter is all about putting everything from the ten previous chapters together. It's just like your birthday. You're giving yourself a gift, a present. Putting everything you want into one box and giving that gift to yourself. By now you should know your passion, and what your goals are, the steps you need to take, and several new tools and ideas to help you along the way.

Back in the day when I was in the mortgage business I was speaking for my company and I did a presentation called putting it all together. I really liked that wrapping it all up into one simple package to get things done. There's something comforting about putting all the pieces of a puzzle together. It's like tying up all those lose ends to get complete. Even if something doesn't work out the way you want it to it's nice to know that if nothing else, it's complete. Again, when you put it all together miraculous things can happen. That time is now. It's time to put everything in this book together so you can create the life you want.

If you use all the tools given to you, you can accomplish anything and everything you want. Please know that you have to use many if not all the things we've given you in this book. Just setting a goal will not be enough. Goals don't just happen because you say I want X. You have to make a plan, then you need to execute on that plan.

Think about the stories and how they relate to you and your life circumstances. Think about your perceptions and the things that have occurred in your life and how they can empower and strengthen you instead of leaving you a victim.

Sometimes life is a series of just rolling with the punches. You never know what's going to happen or when or how it can change your life, and sometimes for the better. This book has given you all the tools, not only to survive the things that happen but to excel past them and come out better, wiser, and stronger on the other side. When and if something occurs that you aren't happy with you can choose what you think and how you feel. Remember chapter nine? You can act or accept what and how you feel. I don't mean that you should deny your feelings and cover them up when bad things happen. I mean feel what you feel and then take a step back. Ask yourself if there is anything you have learned. Ask yourself, "How can this experience make me a better person?"

Remember the story about not getting the promotion I was up for? That was one of those life changing moments. I could have fallen victim to that event and allowed it to defeat me. I took a stand and said "NO! I am not going to sit back and let this defeat me. I am not going to feel sorry for myself and let this stop me from accomplishing all that I am capable of. This company doesn't see my potential and my hard work then it is up to me to find one that does. I am going to use this to make me stronger and smarter." And I did. I realized the importance of education, something I didn't value years before. I went to vocational school to improve my skills and registered at a community college to start working on my degree. I changed jobs and started working for a company who did respect my work ethic and rewarded me for it.

I have made a lot of mistakes. I didn't make the cheerleading squad, I dropped out of high school, I was married at 21 and divorced at 22. I've been fired from a job and passed up for promotions, I've walked away from things I should have stayed in and I've stayed when I should have walked away. I have learned a lot of lessons and still have many more to come. Everything that happens to me I use to make me stronger. Sometimes it takes a little time to work past these things. Often you have to feel the pain and sadness. That's ok. Feel it, then think about it. Ask, "What have I learned? How can I be better because of this? What good can I do or bring from this?" I can tell you not much gets me down for very long now because I find a way to use that experience to make me a stronger better person.

When I first started applying all the things that I have shared with you, I was confused and had no idea what to do than just stumble along until I figured things out. I went back and forth for over a year when I was thinking about getting out of Corporate America, and boy did I get criticized. I had people tell me I was crazy, stupid, and out of my mind. I let all those words get to me and it stopped me from making a move. I let everyone else's opinions interfere with my gut. I procrastinated on living my dream and following my passion because of what other people said. So I took some baby steps. I did just one little thing at a time. I first wrote down what I wanted. That was my first step to leave Corporate America and follow my passion of speaking and writing. Then I did step two, I made a plan. Yes doubts and fear came up every now and again. Things would happen that would make me wonder if I had done the right thing. I would then use all the other tools to get past that moment of doubt. I would write affirmations and look at my visual map. I would ask myself if the fear were bigger and stronger than me. And if I did fail would my life be over? Would I end up with broken bones? No and no again. Every day I used one or more of the tools that you have been given here. Every day I still do. I remember saying to myself over and over again, "Just do this Shar. If it doesn't work out the way you want, at least you tried and you will have no regrets. Just do this."

Another great example of this is an event that occurred in August 2008. I had a friend whose birthday was August 4th. We spoke on the phone and he said he was having a tough time being 41 years old. We hung up we went on with our day. Over the next few days we had our usual text or email exchange. Ten days later I answered my phone with excitement as I could tell from caller id that it was a mutual friend of the one that just had a birthday, and we hadn't spoken in months. Seconds later my life changed. The words "Shar, I'm sorry I hate to have to tell you this, but Tommy was found dead this morning." A second later I was on my knees in tears. How? What happened? Just days before he was alive and we were on the phone and everything was fine. And now, one of my very best friends is dead.

To this day, we still are not sure what happened. Someone who I'd know for over ten years and spoke to or made contact with almost every day was using crystal meth. How did I not know? How could l call someone a close, dear and best friend and not know something like that was going on. He was given a "hot shot". A lethal combination of drugs generally given with the intent to kill. Who gave it to him or why, we still do not and may not ever know.

Every day for months I cried. Still do, not everyday but sometimes. For weeks I didn't know what to do. I was overwhelmed with sadness that someone I loved was no longer here. What do I do with this? This just feels rotten. How could anything good possibly come of this? Then I decided I wasn't going to be a victim to this. I would use it to do something good. What would I do, I don't know yet. But I would do something.

The next day I wrote down what I had and didn't like, which was this awful and empty feeling. Then I wrote what I wanted in its place. I wrote that I wanted to do something good with the tragedy of Tommy's death. I left it alone for a little while. That night I laid down and asked Tommy what I was supposed to do. I closed my eyes and FFAD came into my head. Join the FFAD and help Friends Fight Against Drugs. The next day a non profit to help make teenagers aware and educated about drug use and the lives it effects, was in process.

Then the plan began. How do I get the word out? How do you create a non profit organization? So, I did some research. I wrote down all that needed to be done. Then I did it. One step at a time. Without fear and without overwhelm, little by little this organization to change lives is being created. Every day I do a little something. Every day I have a little bit of fear about what I am creating and how to deal with something I know very little about. I think about what I feel and how I make it real. I feel great when I think about the non profit that will do so much good. I just know it will be real. I made a choice to not be a victim to this tragedy. As awful as it was I chose to do something good with it. I chose to accept what happened even though I didn't like it and then I chose to take action and do something about it.

A few weeks after I decided to create this charity a very interesting thing happened. I got in a taxi to go to the airport. It was extremely early around 4:30 in the morning. The driver was very chatty, telling me about his daughter and how wonderful she was. She went to a private high school on a scholarship and went to an Ivy League college also on a full scholarship. She always got great grades and worked hard to achieve things. She had traveled after graduation to do some charity work. When she returned she committed suicide. Twenty years old with a very bright future in front of her, she took her own life.

This man was clearly distraught. He said he had lost the will to live and he too wanted to take his life. His daughter was everything and he had no idea how to live without her. After a moment of silence caused by shock and disbelief, I told him what had happened to my friend. How I had no idea what to do after he died. I said I know that in no way does this remotely compare to his daughter but I shared with him the charity that I was creating to help this from happening to anyone else. I said "I won't pretend to know the pain you must feel. I can't begin to fathom for a moment how horrible this must be for you. But I beg you to do something good with this. Share her story to help other parents from ever having to go through this. Create a foundation or a charity to reach other young adults and parents. Please do something positive with this catastrophe."

He was silent for the last few minutes of the drive. When we got to the airport he took my suitcase to the curb. After a second he shook my hand and said, "Thank you. I'm very glad I met you. I was meant to pick you up today."

I would not have known what to say to this person a few months before. When it happened I still had no idea what to say or do. However, after dealing with my friend's death I was able to say something that had some effect on this man. I have no idea where he went or what if anything he has done. But in my heart I believe he is doing something good with his tragedy. Maybe my tragedy was to help me help this man. I don't know why it happened, but I know my choices on how to deal with it are far more important.

Again, we have no idea what is going to happen to us or why. But all things, good and bad can make you stronger and better. However, you must choose that path. There is a lot of responsibility in our choices. We may not choose what happens to us, but we do choose what we do with what happens to us.

Several years ago I was watching a baseball game and I had a very interesting epiphany. I had had a very rough day at work and was watching TV to get away from it all. I don't remember which teams were playing but I remember watching the pitcher throw the ball to the batter. The batter chooses if he is going to swing. He doesn't have to swing, but he can if he chooses to. All the sudden I realized, just because someone throws you a ball you don't have to catch it.

I have had many a bad things said to me and about me. Let me tell you being a woman in a male dominated business can be a tough thing to handle. When I was doing very well, I had women and men saying bad things about me. Even after I left the business and was doing well and had articles or interviews done on me in magazines and newspapers, there were negative and horrible things said and written about me. Comments from people who didn't know me at all were saying slanderous and malicious things. It was terrible to read comments from people I don't even know. Of course on the flip side, I have had several experiences where people in my family have said horrible and unkind things to me. Even my husband when I was married called me a name that still stings when I think about it.

Tip #41- Tough times never last, tough people do.
(quote from Dr. Robert H. Schuller)

Another example, I was once dating a man that worked for the same company I did. I ended things between us because I had some loose ends to tie up. I later found out he had cheated on me. When I confronted him he admitted it. I let him know that there was no getting back together now, he closed that coffin and buried it six feet under. Later, he decided to hack into my email and found a correspondence with someone new. Someone who was weeks after our breakup. He went to my boss and told him I cheated on him and do they want someone like that representing our company. I was removed from my position and this little tale traveled throughout my corporate office. My reputation never recovered. I did not deserve that at all. This man cheated on me and I moved on and was judged and sentence for a crime I didn't commit. Did I deserve that? No, I didn't. That is just one example of bad things happen to good people. Sometimes things that happen aren't fair, but they still happen.

What did I do, well I learned. I learned that business is business and pleasure is pleasure and the two don't have to cross. I'm sure you have heard the phrase don't pee in the company pool, well that was a lesson I didn't need to learn twice. From that point forward I no longer mix business and pleasure.

Tip #42- Sometimes mixing business and pleasure, isn't a good mix.

I could go on and on with all the examples from my life and from the lives of those I know and have worked with. Sometimes life isn't fair, it's what you do with what comes at you that matters.

You now know what to do AND how to do it. From there, its all up to you.

Tip #43- Be clear. Start right now. Here's how.

Exercise 11.1

Step 1. Write down what you want to change. Again, start with what you have and don't want or like.

Step 2. Write down what your passion is. What makes you feel great? What makes time fly by in what feels like a second?

Step 3. Write down one thing, just one thing that you want. Write down one goal that you can and will start working on right now.

Step 4. Write down the steps you need to get from Point A, where you are right now, to Point B, where you want to be. Break it down, and dice it into little things you can do everyday.

Step 5. Write down what you are afraid of. Ask yourself is this fear real or fake. Ask yourself "what do I really have to lose." Likely nothing. Even if it is something, what's worse, the fear coming true or going through life without trying and wondering what if?

Step 6. Write down how it would feel to have what you want. Close your eyes and imagine your life and everything in it exactly as you want it to be. Then feel. Feel the joy, happiness, excitement, etc. What you feel, now go make real.

Step 7. Write down the choices you are making right now to change the life you have to get the life you want. Choose it now. Choose to be the change.

Step 8. Write down what you are committed to right now. Write a contract and sign it. Then write how you are going to communicate it. Write down how you are going to share it with everyone you know. Then do it. Three C's. Commit, Communicate and Create

Step 9. Write down what you have perpetually been complaining about. Then write down what action you are going to take or what you are going to stop complaining about right now and accept. Again, it's all about your choices. Act or Accept.

Step 10. Find out why you are procrastinating and deal with it so you can move past it.

Step 11. Do. You have now done all the work in 10 simple steps. Just do. Starting now.

There it is. Everything you need in 11 simple steps. It isn't complicated and doesn't need to be. One step at a time. You can do this! Whatever you have set out for, you can be, do or have it. You must believe in yourself. You must take action.

Tip #44- You have what it takes. Trust, believe, and take action.

Exercise11.2

1. Write down steps 1 through 11. Be clear, be honest, and do it.

LESSONS LEARNED

1. Know what you want.
2. Take it one step at a time.
3. Face your fears.
4. Believe in yourself.
5. Take action!

Conclusion

This is part that I used to hate. When the end of the book was near and it was time to take action. "But I don't know where to start. I don't know what to do? There was so much information that I can't possibly remember what to do with it all." Here is where so many, read the last lines, close the cover and put it on the shelf never to be seen again just like all those goals and dreams. On a shelf somewhere, gathering dust. Well not this time, not this book.

This is where everything comes together. This is where you take action and I'm going to help you. Success is a choice. Having the life you want is a choice. This is all up to you. You can do anything and everything you want, but yes, you must take action.

Starting here, starting now you must take accountability and responsibility for where you are. It doesn't matter why or how you got there, you are there. You are just the spot on the map that reads "you are here." You are here. So what are you going to do with it now?

You are going to make a choice. You are going to choose the life you have or the life you want. It all begins with you. You have already done the work. You have read the words on these pages. There are exercises that were designed to walk you through step by step. You can change your life and you can start right now.

That's all folks. Life isn't that complicated if we break things down into little bite sized pieces. Put it all together now. Find what you are passionate about, make the plan, use visual maps and trigger devices and the 3 C's, etc to get what you want. You not only have a firearm in your cabinet you have a whole arsenal! Use them and use them all to create the life you want now.

Bonus

To get your free bonus go to <u>www.wowandthehow/bonus</u>. There you will receive:

- Downloadable two hour audiobook with additional coaching tips and advice to help you find your WOW and learn HOW to get what you want.

- Giving you the WOW home study workbook where you can do written exercises to take your life to the next level.

BUY A SHARE OF THE FUTURE IN YOUR COMMUNITY

These certificates make great holiday, graduation and birthday gifts that can be personalized with the recipient's name. The cost of one S.H.A.R.E. or one square foot is $54.17. The personalized certificate is suitable for framing and will state the number of shares purchased and the amount of each share, as well as the recipient's name. The home that you participate in "building" will last for many years and will continue to grow in value.

Here is a sample SHARE certificate:

YES, I WOULD LIKE TO HELP!

*I support the work that Habitat for Humanity does and I want to be part of the excitement! As a donor, I will receive periodic updates on your construction activities but, more importantly, I know my gift will help a family in our community realize the dream of homeownership. **I would like to SHARE in your efforts against substandard housing in my community!** (Please print below)*

PLEASE SEND ME _____ SHARES at $54.17 EACH = $ $_____

In Honor Of: _____

Occasion: (Circle One)   HOLIDAY   BIRTHDAY   ANNIVERSARY

            OTHER: _____

Address of Recipient: _____

Gift From: _____   *Donor Address:* _____

Donor Email: _____

I AM ENCLOSING A CHECK FOR $ $_____ PAYABLE TO HABITAT FOR HUMANITY OR PLEASE CHARGE MY VISA OR MASTERCARD *(CIRCLE ONE)*

Card Number _____   Expiration Date: _____

Name as it appears on Credit Card _____   Charge Amount $ _____

Signature _____

Billing Address _____

Telephone # Day _____   Eve _____

PLEASE NOTE: Your contribution is tax-deductible to the fullest extent allowed by law.
Habitat for Humanity • P.O. Box 1443 • Newport News, VA 23601 • 757-596-5553
www.HelpHabitatforHumanity.org

Breinigsville, PA USA
01 June 2010

238963BV00002B/1/P